Contents

Introduction

The human body is a fascinating and remarkable machine. Its design is far more complex than the most advanced computer. The achievements of athletes demonstrate its suppleness and stamina, while the mental powers of a chess grand master show the immense capacity of the brain.

Deep inside, the body is still more impressive. Billions of cells carry out thousands of different functions. Without our conscious knowledge, the body regulates its own temperature, water content, the digestion of food, the rate of the heartbeat and numerous other processes. The coordinating centre for all these activities is the brain. It receives, records and stores a greater variety of data than any computer ever could. To understand how the body and brain work, we must examine them bit by bit. As we consider the body and brain together, we can begin to appreciate their complexity.

◄ Inside a human bone. These fluid-filled bone cells have spaces between them; spongy bone is not solid. It is in other spaces that the vital bone marrow is found. Bone marrow produces blood cells.

The human frame

- A baby has about 350 individual bones but an adult only 206. As the skeleton grows some of its smaller bones join to form larger ones.

- Part of the dust in your home is dead skin cells from you and your family.

- There are about 200 different joints in a human body.

- The whole skin has an area of about 2 square metres. In total, it weighs about 3 kg.

▶ The movements of a gymnast demonstrate how the muscles, bones and brain work together. A smooth performance like this depends on muscle strength so the body can move without jerking. The brain is in overall control, receiving messages from the nerve endings in feet and hands and from the eyes. The gymnast's balance depends on a mechanism in the ear.

Every move you make, from the smallest flicker of an eyelid to the greatest leap into the air, depends upon your muscles and bones. The same is true of every breath you take. Without muscles you would be unable to move, and would remain still and lifeless. Without the bones of your skeleton your body could not stay upright and you would collapse in a heap.

While your skeleton holds your body together and supports its weight, your muscles work together to bend it at your joints, so that your movements are smooth and supple. Your muscles and bones are covered, enclosed and protected by your skin. This is a flexible, living coating that never wears out.

Skin

Skin has an outer, dead surface which is constantly being rubbed away, but it never wears out. Just beneath its outer surface, skin has two main layers which are very much alive. The epidermis makes up the top half-millimetre or so. Beneath this is the dermis, about two millimetres thick. Millions of dividing cells at the base of the epidermis push wave after wave of new cells up towards the surface. Closer to the surface, they are squashed flat and die. This flexible pavement of dead cells is waterproof.

The dermis gives the skin its strength and ability to stretch. It is here that vital nerves, glands, hairs and blood vessels are to be found. Skin contains millions of sensitive nerve endings which tell the brain about touch, temperature, pressure and pain. Around three million glands will produce sweat to cool the body if it becomes too hot. Sebaceous glands produce an oil called sebum, which keeps the skin supple and waterproof.

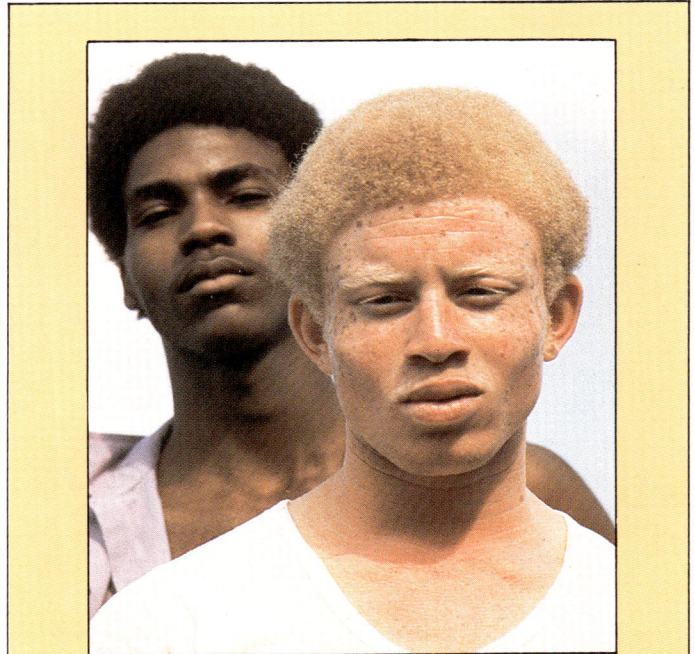

Skin pigment

Albinos have very white skin and hair, and very pale eyes. They lack the pigment melanin which gives skin its dark colour and protects it from the Sun's harmful rays.

The skin

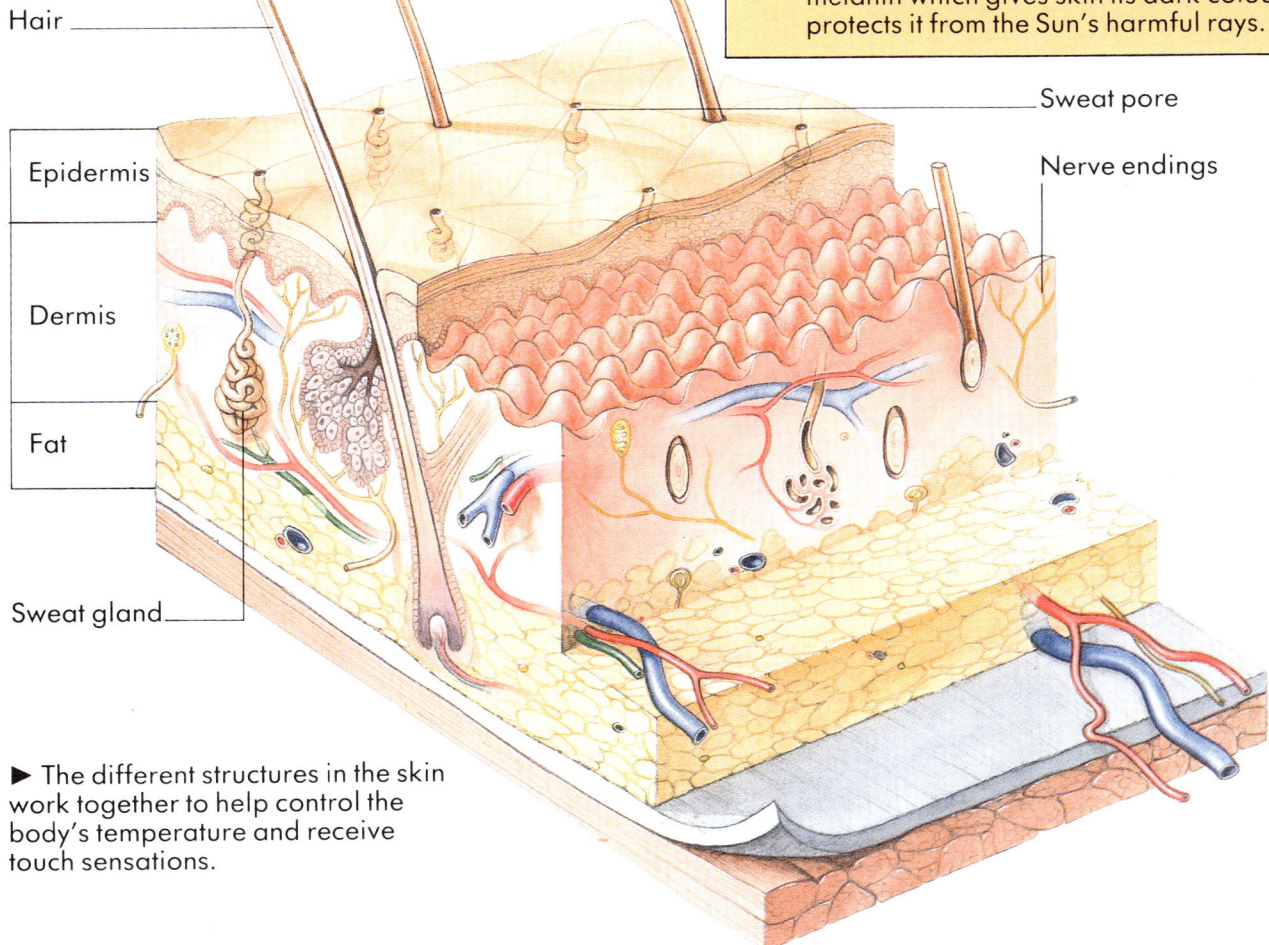

Hair

Epidermis

Dermis

Fat

Sweat gland

Sweat pore

Nerve endings

▶ The different structures in the skin work together to help control the body's temperature and receive touch sensations.

The skeleton

The skeleton

Skull

Jaw bone

Shoulder blade

Collar bone

Ribs

Backbones

Femur

Knee cap

Tibia

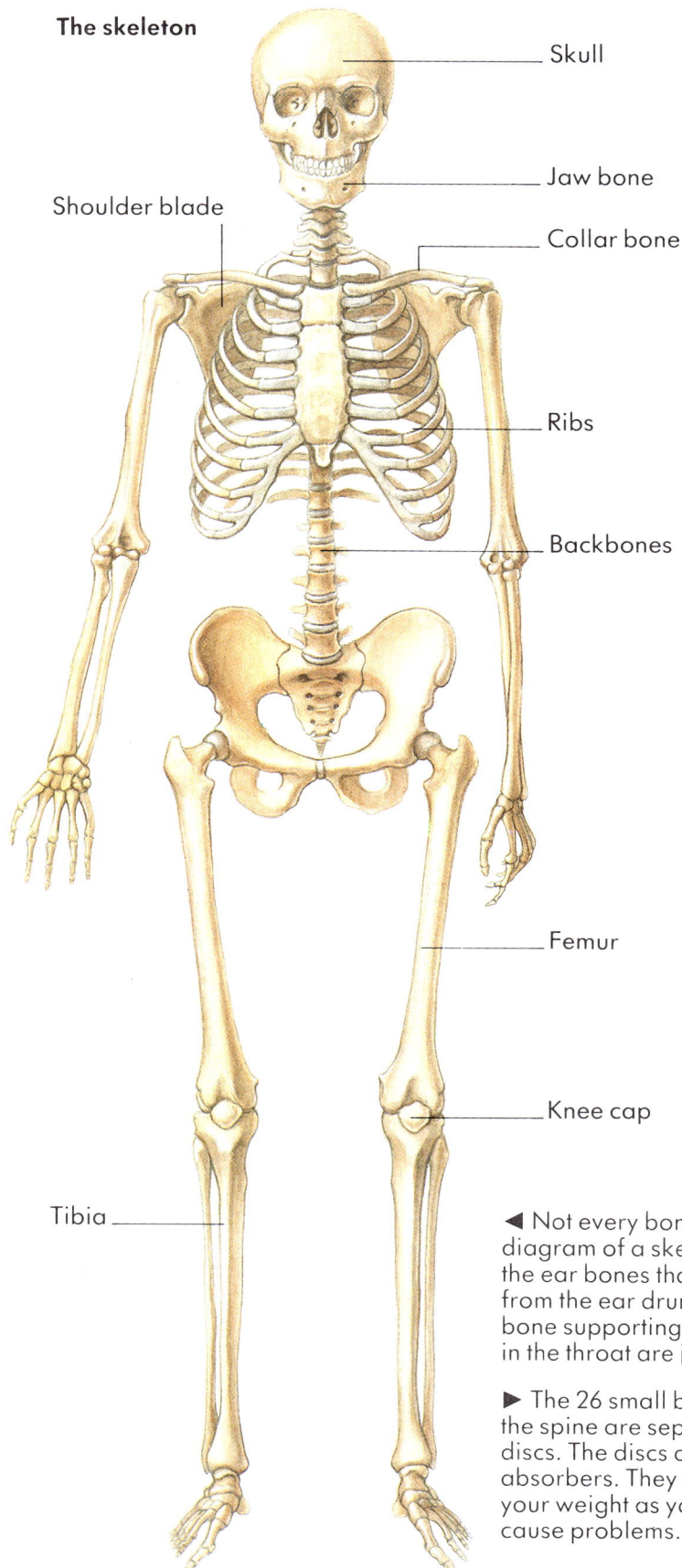

The skeleton gives the body its internal framework. Bone is a perfect construction material, combining great strength with light weight. Bones help to protect the body's soft organs. The dish-shaped hip bones enclose the intestines and bladder, while the ribs and backbone form a cage around the heart and lungs. These bones protect the vital organs from everyday knocks and bumps.

An adult has 206 bones, although some people may have extra ribs or bones in their fingers. Of these, 26 bones make up the spine, each arm has 32 bones and each leg 31. The largest bones are the femurs or thigh bones which account for around a quarter of the skeleton's body weight. The smallest bone, only 3 mm long, is the stirrup bone in the ear.

Without bones we could not move for it is bones which muscles pull into place when we change position. Many bones have flat surfaces which provide an anchorage for large muscles. Some bones have projections from them to which muscles are attached. One example is the shoulder blade which provides anchorage for several muscles, which work together to move the arm and shoulder.

The backbone

7 neck bones

12 thoracic bones

5 lumbar bones

Sacral curve

1 coccyx

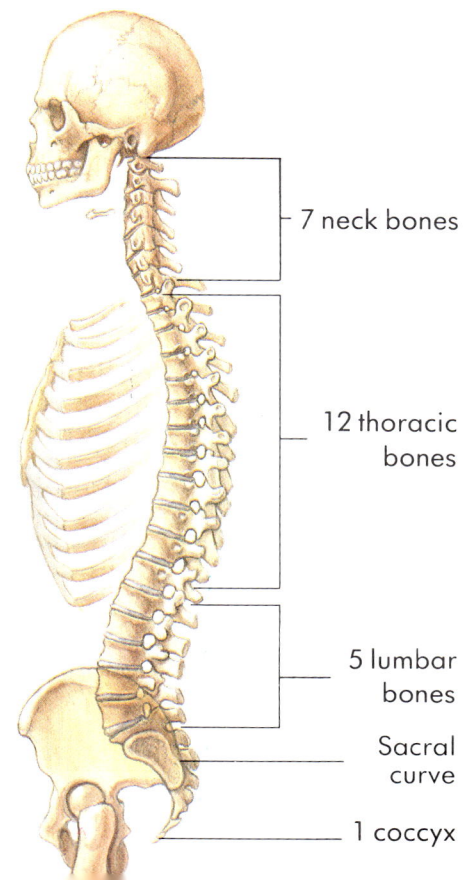

◄ Not every bone can be shown in a diagram of a skeleton. For example, the ear bones that transmit sounds from the ear drum, and the hyoid bone supporting the tongue muscles in the throat are just too small.

► The 26 small bones that make up the spine are separated by cartilage discs. The discs act as shock absorbers. They are squashed by your weight as you walk, and can cause problems.

Living bone contains large quantities of three important minerals: calcium, phosphorus and potassium. These substances give bone its strength and hardness but they are also needed in other vital processes such as sending messages along the nerves. If a person's diet does not contain enough of these minerals, the body can use the stores it has locked up in bones. This may weaken bones for a time until the stores can be replenished.

Bone is alive, and continues to grow as the body matures. If a bone breaks it is able to mend itself by producing new cells. Bones can also strengthen themselves if a person is very active so their bones can stand up to extra stresses and strains. In a less active person bones do not need to be so strong and the calcium that gives bone its hardness can be gradually dissolved away.

The skull

Eye socket

Upper jaw

Lower jaw

Hyoid bone

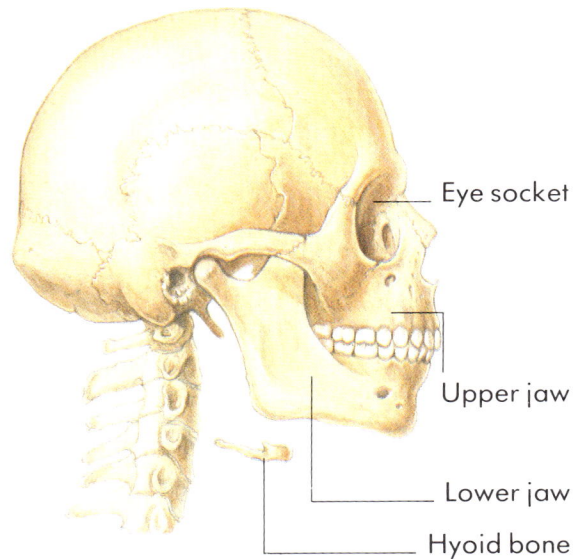

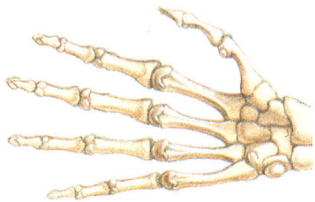

◀ The unique arrangement of bones in a human hand gives us the ability to touch the tip of each finger with our thumb. This means we can perform delicate tasks like threading a needle or coordinated activities such as holding a pen and unscrewing its top with just one hand. Other animals cannot do this.

▲ The skull forms a hard case which protects the brain. A new born baby has 29 separate bones forming its skull. These overlap as the baby is born but gradually fuse firmly together during the first two years of life. Only the lower jaw remains a separate, moving part, making it possible for food to be chewed.

Inside a bone

Blood vessel

Compact bone

Cartilage

Spongy bone

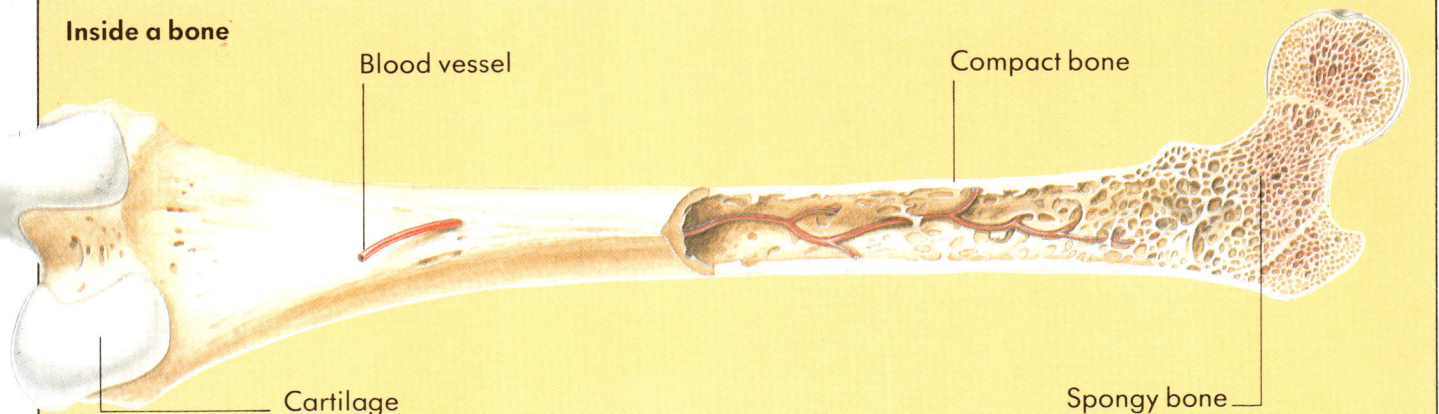

Bones are not solid. Long bones like the femur have a hard, strong outer layer of compact bone which surrounds lightweight spongy bone inside. A network of blood vessels and nerves runs in canals through these outer bone layers to the hollow centre of bone marrow. The canals also carry lymph vessels.

Bone marrow produces millions of red blood cells every day. Most of our bones contain marrow when we are children, but as we get older the marrow-producing red cells are only to be found in the skull, backbone, hip and some limb bones. There is a photograph of bone marrow cells on the front cover.

Muscles and joints

The muscles

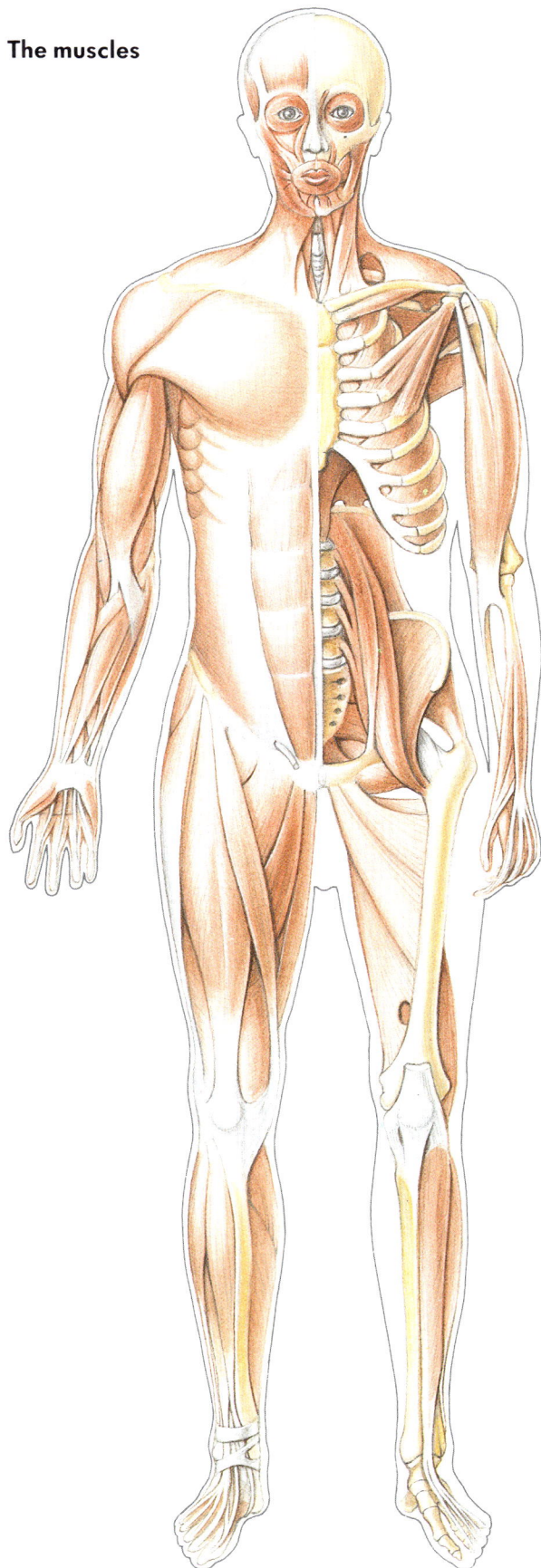

Bones are rigid and cannot bend, but where two bones meet a joint is formed. Joints allow us to bend, twist or turn. There are more than 200 joints in the body. Each one allows a particular type or degree of movement.

Hinge-like joints allow limited movement: for example the elbow permits the lower arm only to move up and down. Ball and socket joints allow turning movements which are more free. Examples are the shoulder and hip joints. Not all joints allow movement. Some, like those in the skull, have bones which meet so closely that there is no gap between them.

The strongest joints are those which allow the least movement, such as those between the bones in the hand. A more flexible joint like the shoulder is weaker and the bones are more likely to be separated or dislocated. Bones are held together by strong fibres called ligaments. At a moving joint, the ends of the bones are covered with smooth, shiny cartilage that reduces the amount of friction between them.

◀ The voluntary muscles which cover the skeleton have two important jobs to do. The first is to produce movement. The second is to keep the body upright. Even when a person is standing still, some of their muscle fibres are contracting. The contraction or "tone" of these muscles gives the body its shape. At the same time, different, "involuntary" muscles automatically keep the heart beating and food moving along the intestine.

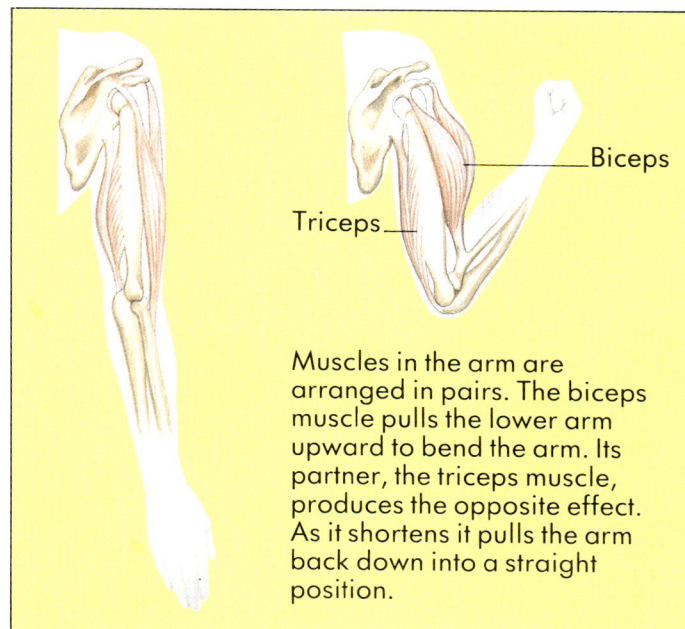

Biceps

Triceps

Muscles in the arm are arranged in pairs. The biceps muscle pulls the lower arm upward to bend the arm. Its partner, the triceps muscle, produces the opposite effect. As it shortens it pulls the arm back down into a straight position.

Pulling on the bones of our skeleton to move us from place to place, we have more than 600 "voluntary" muscles. They are known as voluntary muscles because we can use them when we want to. But each muscle is not controlled individually. They work in groups under the control of the brain. An action such as raising a leg involves not only the muscles in the leg, but also a series of muscles in the back and hips which adjust the balance and position of the rest of the body.

Muscles are anchored to bones by tendons. When a muscle contracts, it pulls on the tendon and this moves the bone. Muscles are arranged in pairs so that there is one muscle to bend a joint with a partner to straighten it again.

Individual muscles are composed of fibres up to 30 cm long. Although we cannot increase the total number of fibres in a muscle, their size increases if they are used regularly. About 42 per cent of a man's weight and 36 per cent of a woman's weight is made up of muscle.

The knee joint

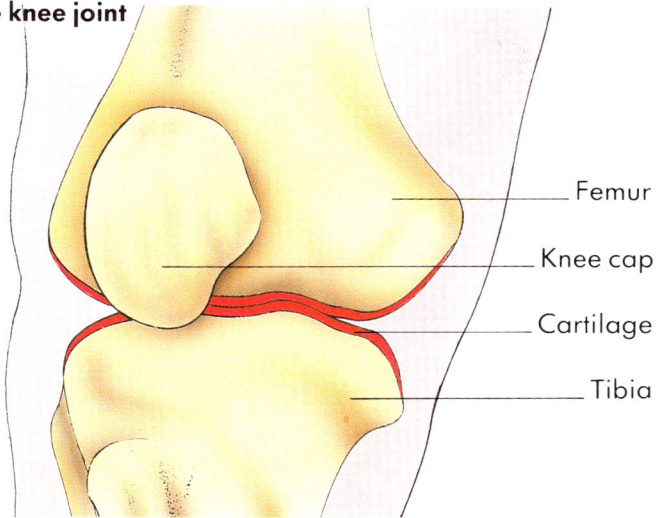

Femur

Knee cap

Cartilage

Tibia

▲ At the knee joint the femur or thigh bone meets the tibia or shin bone. The joint moves smoothly because the cartilage-covered ends of the bones are separated by a thin layer of lubricating fluid. The fluid is produced by the synovial membrane which encloses and protects the joint. The kneecap provides further protection.

Joints

Pivot joint

Hinge joint

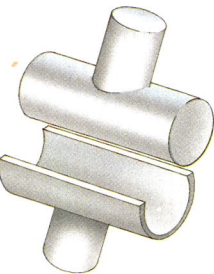

◀ These joints each produce a different type of movement. The pivot joint allows the head to turn. Hinge joints allow bending at the knee and elbow. At the wrist and ankle ellipsoidal joints can turn and bend, while ball and socket joints allow circular movements of the hip.

Neck

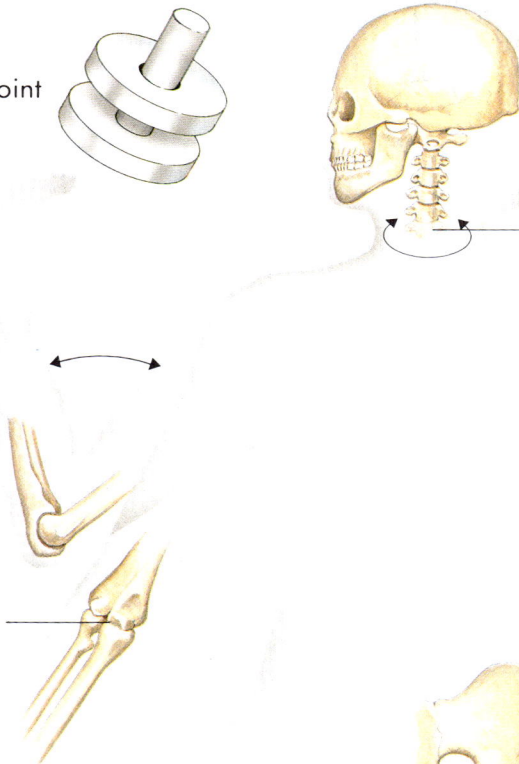

Elbow

Ball and socket joint

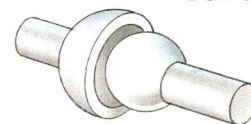

Ellipsoidal joint

Hip

Wrist

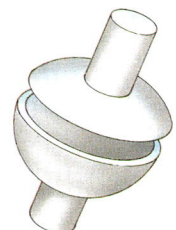

The circulation

Spot facts

- One drop of blood contains 1,000 million red blood cells and 2 million white blood cells.

- A woman's body contains between 4 and 5 litres of blood; a man's has 5 to 6 litres.

- Your heart is about the size of your clenched fist. An average heart weighs around 300 g.

- Your heart beats about 40 million times every year.

- The heart of a young baby beats up to 120 times every minute.

Just as a city needs transport to carry people and goods to and from homes, factories and shops, so our bodies need an internal transport system. In the body, this system has to distribute food and nutrients, to carry oxygen and to remove waste. The body's transport network is its blood system. It consists of an extensive series of branching tubes, called blood vessels, containing a life-sustaining fluid – blood.

The network of blood vessels reaches every part of the body and the blood flowing through it brings vital nutrients and oxygen to every cell. The driving force at the centre of the system is the heart, which is a strong pump. This beats continuously, day and night, without our ever having to think about it.

► This boy is having his blood pressure measured. Blood pressure is the pressure of blood against the walls of the main arteries. The pressure is highest when the ventricles of the heart contract. It is lowest when the ventricles are relaxing and refilling with blood. Blood pressure is measured at an artery in the arm where the pressure is most similar to that of blood leaving the heart.

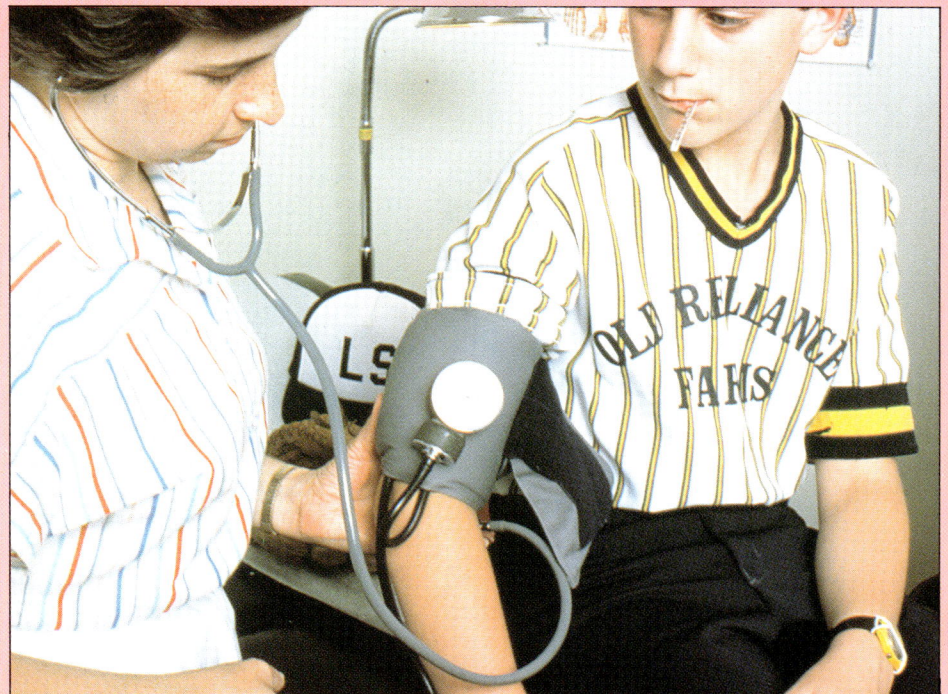

The blood system

The network of vessels through which blood flows is more than 100,000 km long. Stretched end to end they would encircle the Earth almost three times. The strongest of all the blood vessels are the arteries which leave the heart and carry blood out to the rest of the body. Their walls must be thick and tough to withstand the high pressure of the blood which surges from the heart each time it beats. Arteries divide and branch to form smaller vessels called arterioles. These also divide many times until they become a mesh of tiny vessels called capillaries.

Capillaries are so small that they fit between body cells and carry blood right into the body's organs. Through their thin walls a transfer takes place. Food and oxygen are delivered to the cells and waste products are taken away.

Capillaries meet up again forming larger vessels called venules. These, in turn, join to form veins which carry blood back to the heart. Blood at this stage of its journey has only low pressure, and so veins are less firm than arteries and have thinner walls. Blood travels slowly along veins. Because the returning blood must often flow upwards through the arms and legs, the larger veins contain valves to ensure that it flows only in one direction.

Veins and arteries

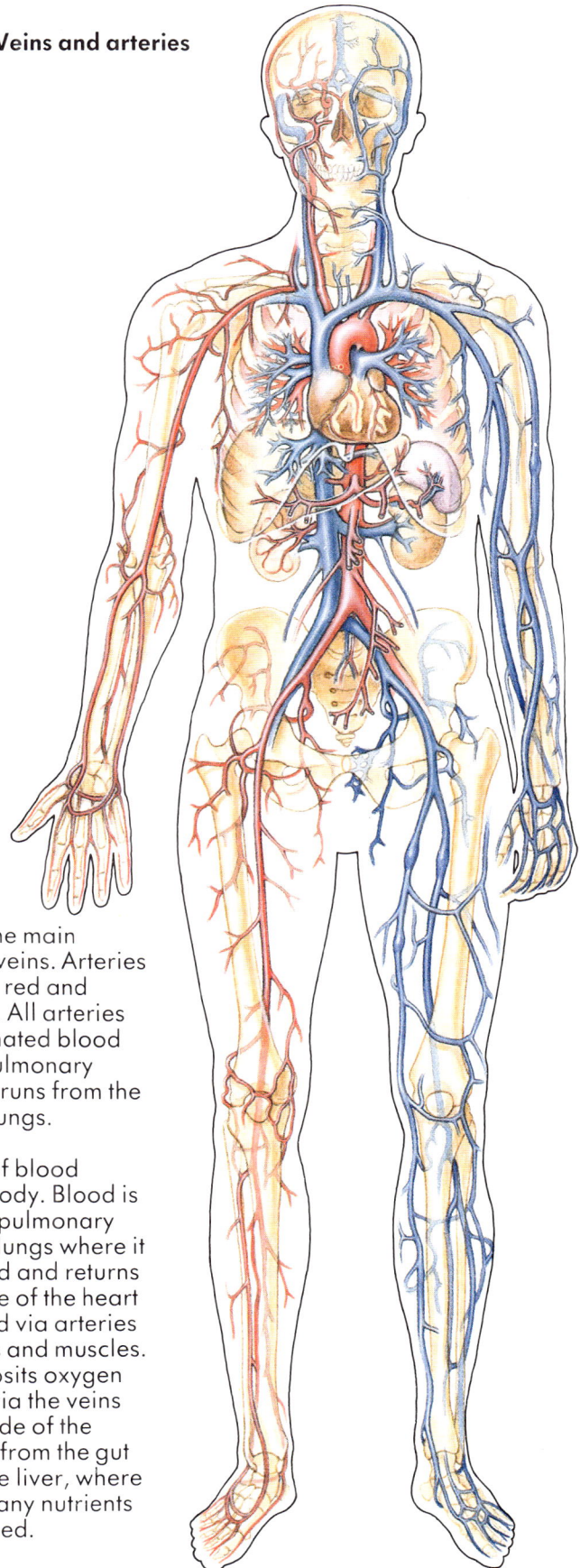

Circulation of the blood

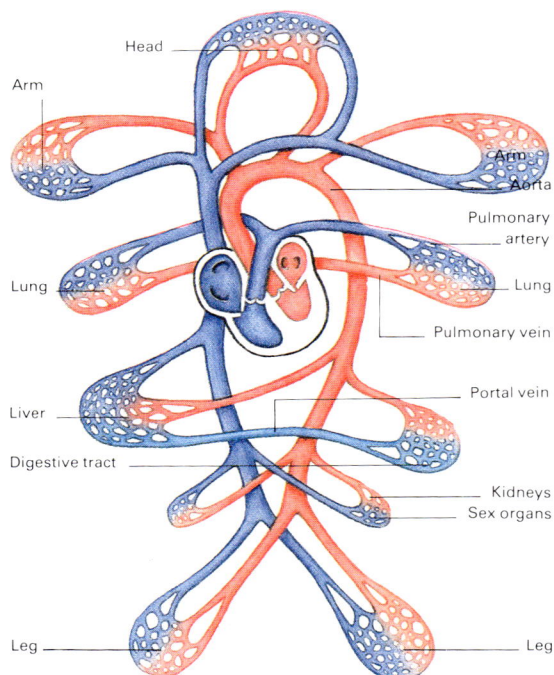

Head
Arm
Arm
Aorta
Pulmonary artery
Lung
Lung
Pulmonary vein
Portal vein
Liver
Digestive tract
Kidneys
Sex organs
Leg
Leg

▶ Some of the main arteries and veins. Arteries are shown in red and veins in blue. All arteries carry oxygenated blood except the pulmonary artery which runs from the heart to the lungs.

◀ The flow of blood around the body. Blood is taken by the pulmonary artery to the lungs where it is oxygenated and returns to the left side of the heart to be pumped via arteries to the organs and muscles. There it deposits oxygen and returns via the veins to the right side of the heart. Blood from the gut travels via the liver, where it deposits many nutrients it has absorbed.

The heart and blood

The heart is made almost entirely of a unique type of involuntary muscle which never tires. In an average lifetime the heart will beat 3,000 million times, about once per second.

A heart has four separate chambers which together form two pumps, side by side. The left hand side of the heart pumps blood all around the body, while the right drives blood to the lungs. Each side of the heart has a smaller, upper chamber or atrium and a lower chamber called a ventricle. The atria each connect through strong valves with the larger, more powerful ventricles. When the ventricles contract they propel blood into the arteries at a speed of 30 cm per second.

The heart of an adult sitting quietly will beat about 70 times per minute, but this can double during vigorous exercise. The heart rate is controlled by the brain through the nervous system, but when we are excited or afraid, the rate can be speeded up by the release of hormones into the bloodstream.

The blood driven along by each heartbeat may seem to be simply a red liquid, but in fact it contains billions of cells floating in a chemical cocktail known as plasma. Red blood cells make up about half the blood's volume. Their job is to carry oxygen and their unusual doughnut shape gives them a huge surface area to absorb it. Red cells pick up oxygen in the lungs where it is abundant and release it in the cells where it is scarce. As well as oxygen, blood carries another gas, carbon dioxide. Produced by cells, this is gathered in plasma and must be returned to the lungs to be disposed of. Blood also contains white blood cells. Fewer in number than red cells, their task is to fight infection caused by invading bacteria and viruses. There are several different types of white cells which operate in different ways. Macrophages surround and engulf bacteria within their cell membranes and digest them. Others make special substances called antibodies which kill the invading bacteria and viruses.

▼ The upper chambers, the atria, have thin walls because they pump blood only to the ventricles. The wall of the left ventricle is thicker than that of the right, since it must pump blood all around the body. Valves control the flow of blood into and out of the ventricles.

The heart

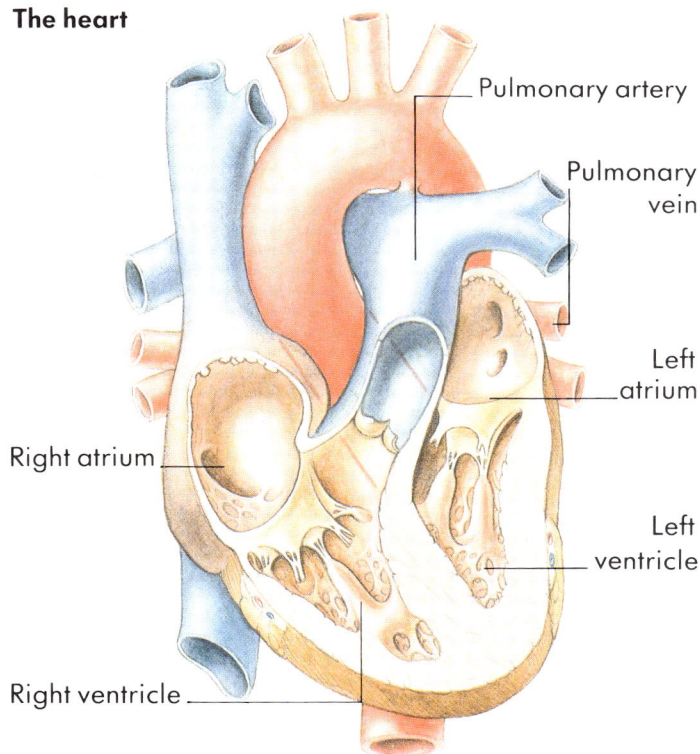

Pulmonary artery

Pulmonary vein

Right atrium

Left atrium

Left ventricle

Right ventricle

The sequence of one complete heartbeat

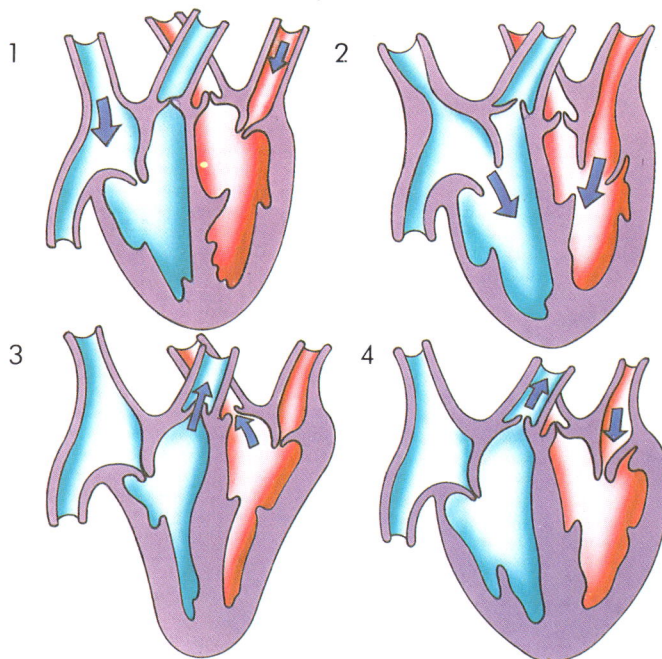

1
2
3
4

▲ (1) Blood from the veins flows into the atria. (2) The atria contract and force blood into the ventricles. (3) Ventricles contract and force blood out into the two main arteries, the aorta and pulmonary artery. (4) The valves in the arteries close and the atria begin to refill with blood.

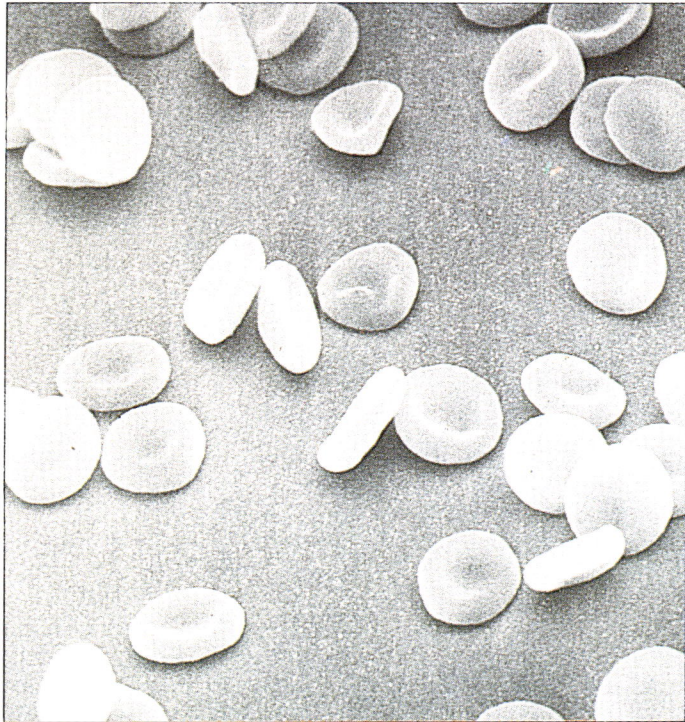

▲ Red blood cells make up nearly half of the blood's volume. Around 55 per cent is plasma, and one tenth of one per cent is white blood cells. There are about 5 million red cells in every millilitre of blood.

▼ A loss of blood through damaged vessels can have serious consequences and so must be dealt with quickly. A mass of fibres is produced which entangles red blood cells in a firm network called a clot. This can seal leaking vessels. The fibres are produced by cell fragments called platelets, which are present in plasma.

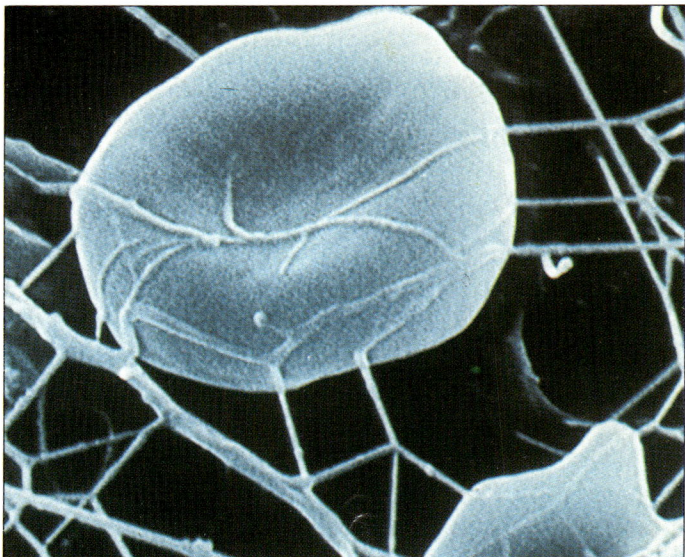

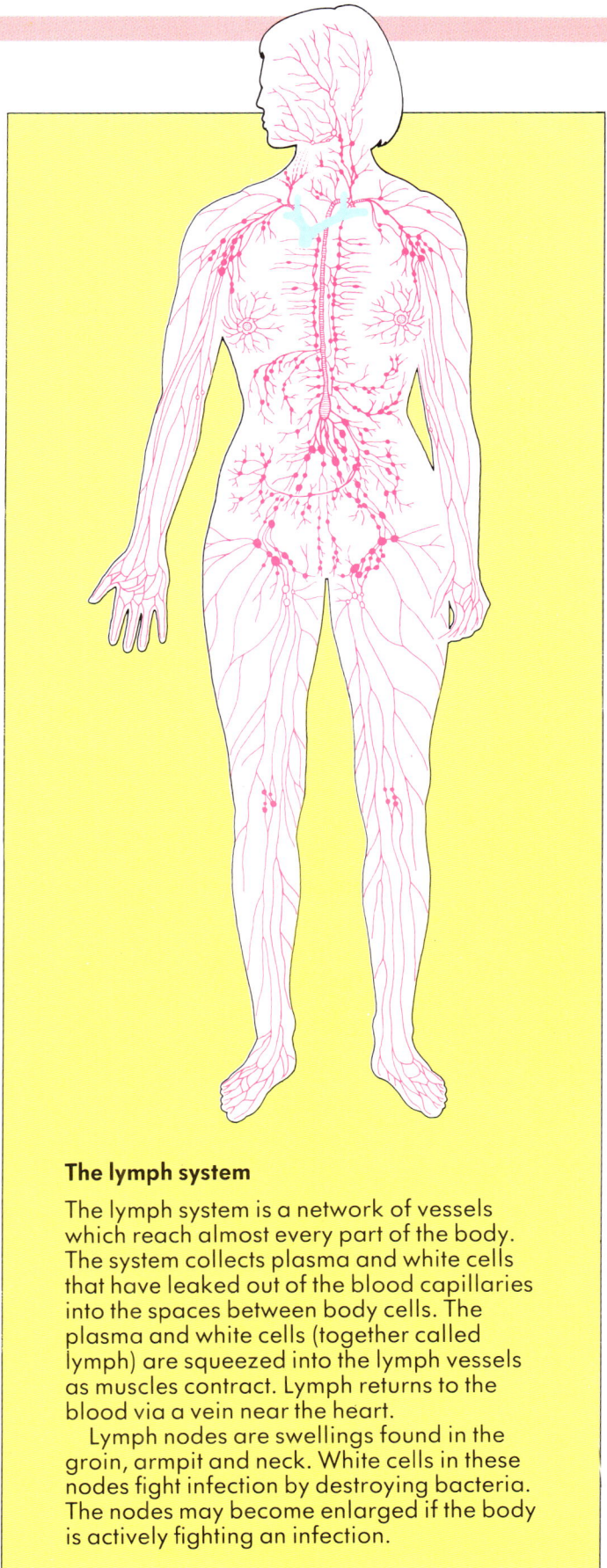

The lymph system

The lymph system is a network of vessels which reach almost every part of the body. The system collects plasma and white cells that have leaked out of the blood capillaries into the spaces between body cells. The plasma and white cells (together called lymph) are squeezed into the lymph vessels as muscles contract. Lymph returns to the blood via a vein near the heart.

Lymph nodes are swellings found in the groin, armpit and neck. White cells in these nodes fight infection by destroying bacteria. The nodes may become enlarged if the body is actively fighting an infection.

Breathing

Your body uses energy to power all the activities of every cell. Energy comes from the food you eat, but is released in cells during respiration, a process which requires a constant supply of oxygen. Your body obtains its oxygen from the air by breathing in and out every few seconds from the moment you are born. The nose, throat, windpipe, lungs and chest muscles together form the breathing system. Their job is to bring oxygen into the body and to remove carbon dioxide, a waste product of respiration.

We breathe in about ten times every minute by moving the muscles between and below the ribs. The diaphragm is a sheet of muscle that separates the upper and lower halves of the body. It pushes downwards as muscles between the ribs lift the rib cage upwards. These movements reduce the amount of pressure on the lungs inside the chest, and air is sucked in through the nose. The nose acts as a filter, trapping dirt on tiny hairs and in sticky mucus. The air is also warmed and moistened before passing through the throat into the windpipe.

At the bottom the windpipe divides into two tubes, one leading to the left and the other to the right lung. Inside the lungs, these tubes, known as bronchi, divide many times to form numerous small passageways. Each one ends in a group of tiny air sacs called alveoli.

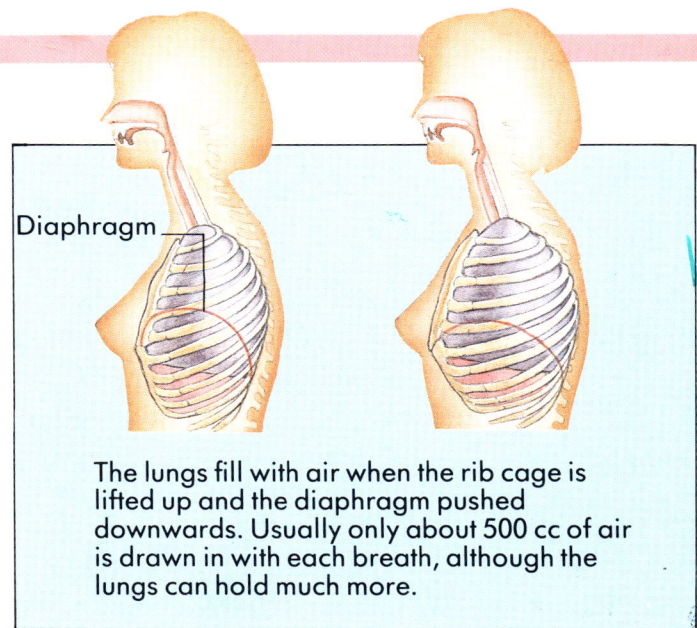

The lungs fill with air when the rib cage is lifted up and the diaphragm pushed downwards. Usually only about 500 cc of air is drawn in with each breath, although the lungs can hold much more.

The respiratory system

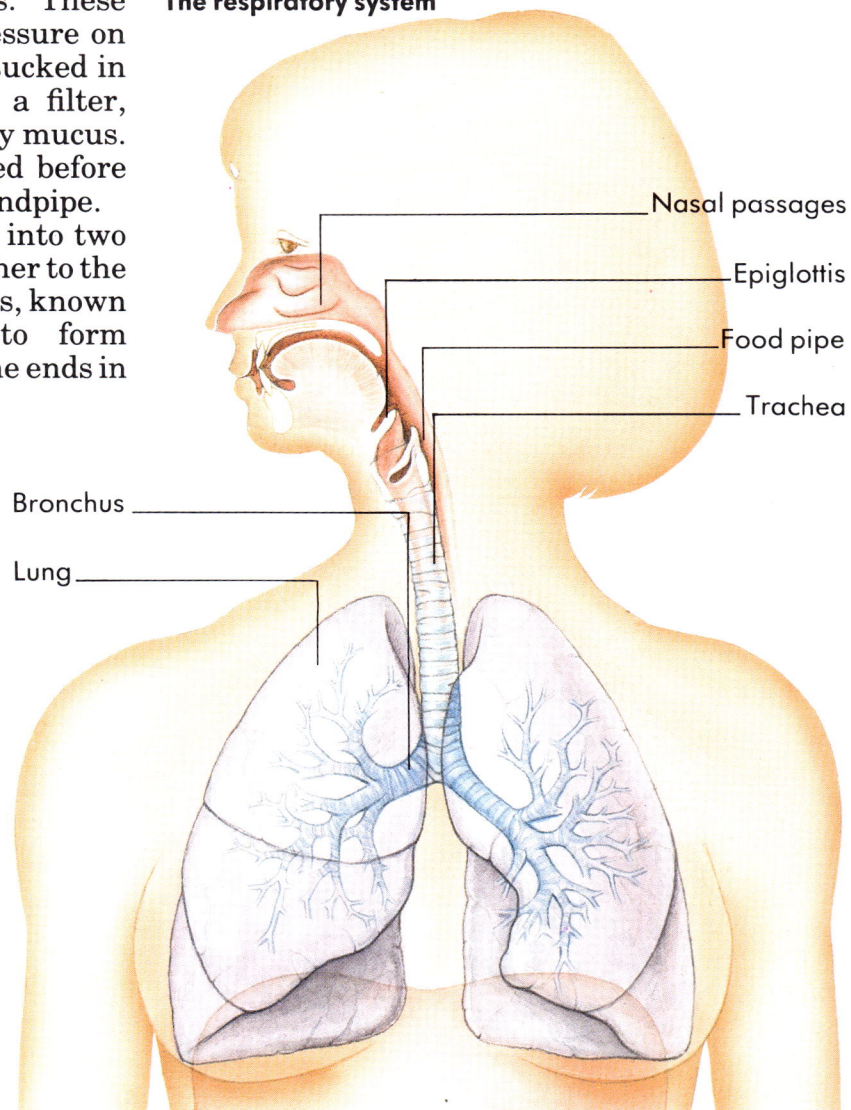

Nasal passages

Epiglottis

Food pipe

Trachea

Bronchus

Lung

▶ Air may enter the lungs either through the nose or the mouth. It passes through the throat into the windpipe, which is held open by a series of cartilage rings. When food is swallowed, the entrance to the windpipe is covered by a flap. This is called the epiglottis and it prevents food going down the "wrong way". The windpipe, bronchi and tiny air passages are kept clean by sticky mucus and wafting hairs, which drive dirt up to the outside.

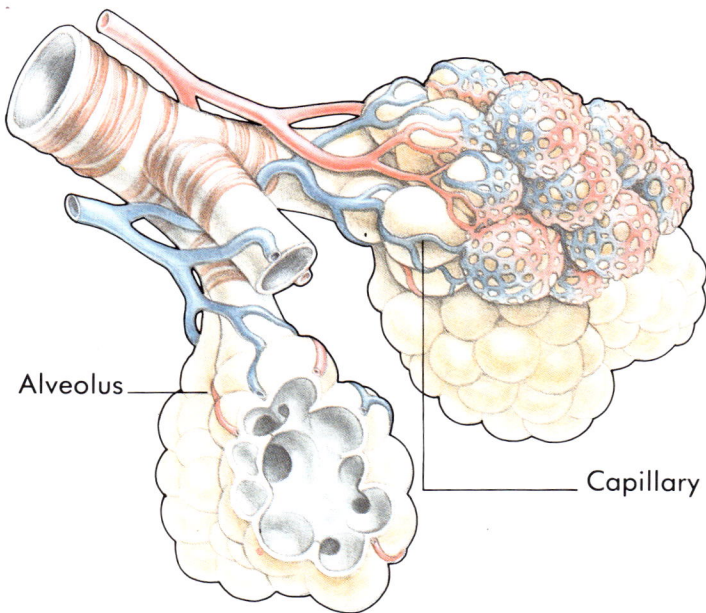

Alveolus — Capillary

▲ Our two lungs have about 600 million alveoli between them. Because lungs are full of these tiny air sacs, they are very light. Each lung has a capacity of 2-3 litres and yet weighs only 1 kg.

Hundreds of millions of alveoli make up the structure of the lungs. It has been estimated that if they were flattened out, the alveoli would cover an area the size of a tennis court. Oxygen passes from the alveoli into the bloodstream so this huge area allows the transfer to take place efficiently. In addition, the walls of the alveoli are very thin and they have a rich blood supply to carry away oxygen. As oxygen enters the blood, carbon dioxide passes in the opposite direction, back into the alveoli. From there it is passed to the lungs.

Breathing out is the reverse of breathing in. Muscles lower the rib cage and the diaphragm is raised. In this way pressure on the lungs is increased and air is driven out.

Normal breathing takes place automatically, although we can control our breathing rate if we want to. Our breathing rate increases considerably during exercise when more oxygen must be supplied to working muscles.

The throat

The larynx or voice box lies at the top of the windpipe. The front of the larynx is protected by a piece of cartilage known as the "Adam's apple". Our ability to speak depends on air passing through the larynx, causing the vocal cords inside to vibrate. The vibration produces a continuous tone. The tone is varied by our moving the muscles in our face, tongue and lips, turning the sound into speech. When muscles in the larynx contract, the cords are pulled tight and the sounds they make become more high-pitched. When the cords are loose, they produce low-pitched sounds. The loudness of the sounds produced depends on how fast the air is pushed past the cords. During normal breathing, the vocal cords do not vibrate or produce sounds.

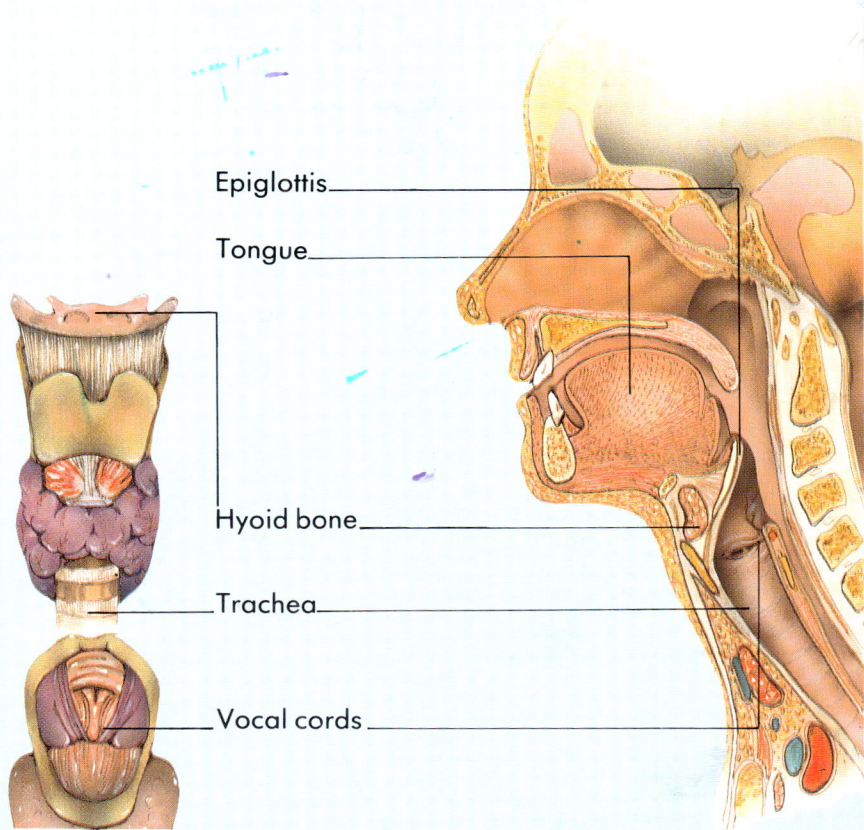

Epiglottis
Tongue
Hyoid bone
Trachea
Vocal cords

The vital molecule

Every red blood cell is packed full of a vital substance, haemoglobin, which is essential to the oxygen-carrying process. There may be 280 million molecules of haemoglobin in every red cell. They act as a go-between, carrying oxygen piggyback fashion from the lungs to body cells. In the lungs haemoglobin combines with molecules of oxygen to form bright red oxy-haemoglobin. On reaching body cells where oxygen is scarce, it releases its load of oxygen and becomes dark blue-red de-oxyhaemoglobin. Each molecule of haemoglobin can carry four molecules of oxygen in this way. Without it, we would probably need 60 times more blood to supply our cells with oxygen.

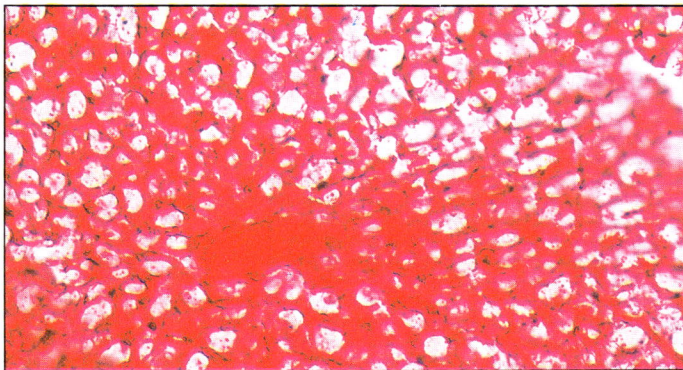

On reaching the cells, oxygen leaves the blood. Along with glucose that has been carried from the digestive system, it passes through the cell membrane. Within the cell, these two substances take part in a series of chemical reactions. These release the energy stored in the glucose molecules so that it can be used to keep the cell alive. The process is known as respiration and takes place in a part of the cell called the mitochondria.

Cells need a constant supply of oxygen to prevent them running out of energy. Brain cells are very sensitive to a shortage of oxygen. If the oxygen supply fails they will begin to die after only three or four minutes.

▲ The network of capillaries found in the liver supplies the large amounts of oxygen and glucose needed for the hundreds of activities that take place here.

▶ Mitochondria are special structures found in every cell. They are the powerhouses that provide the energy to drive all the cells' activities. Not all the energy that is released is used immediately; some may be stored to be used later. Glucose used in the respiration process may come directly from the digestive system or it may come from stores that are held in the liver and muscles. Water is produced and enters the bloodstream as waste.

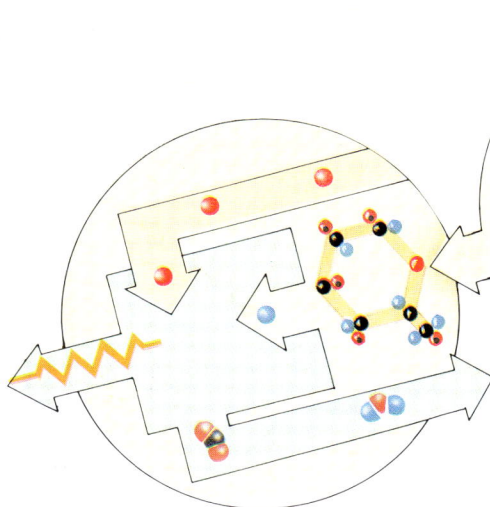

How haemoglobin works

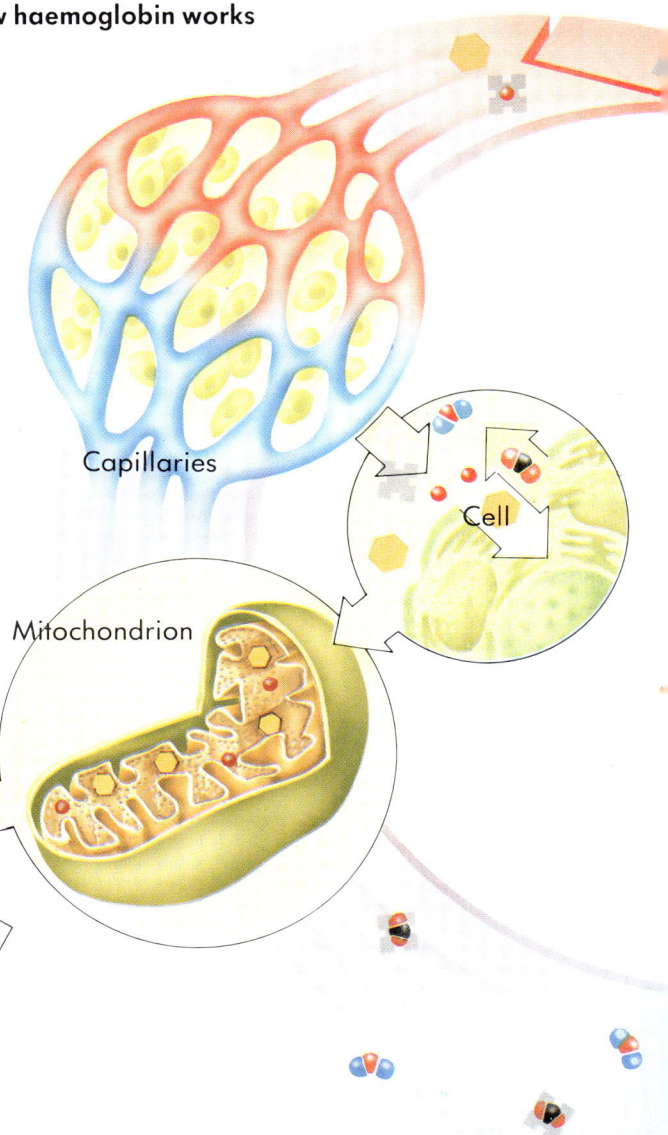

Capillaries

Cell

Mitochondrion

Lung

Capillaries

Alveoli

Veins

Arteries

Heart

Arteries

Alveolus

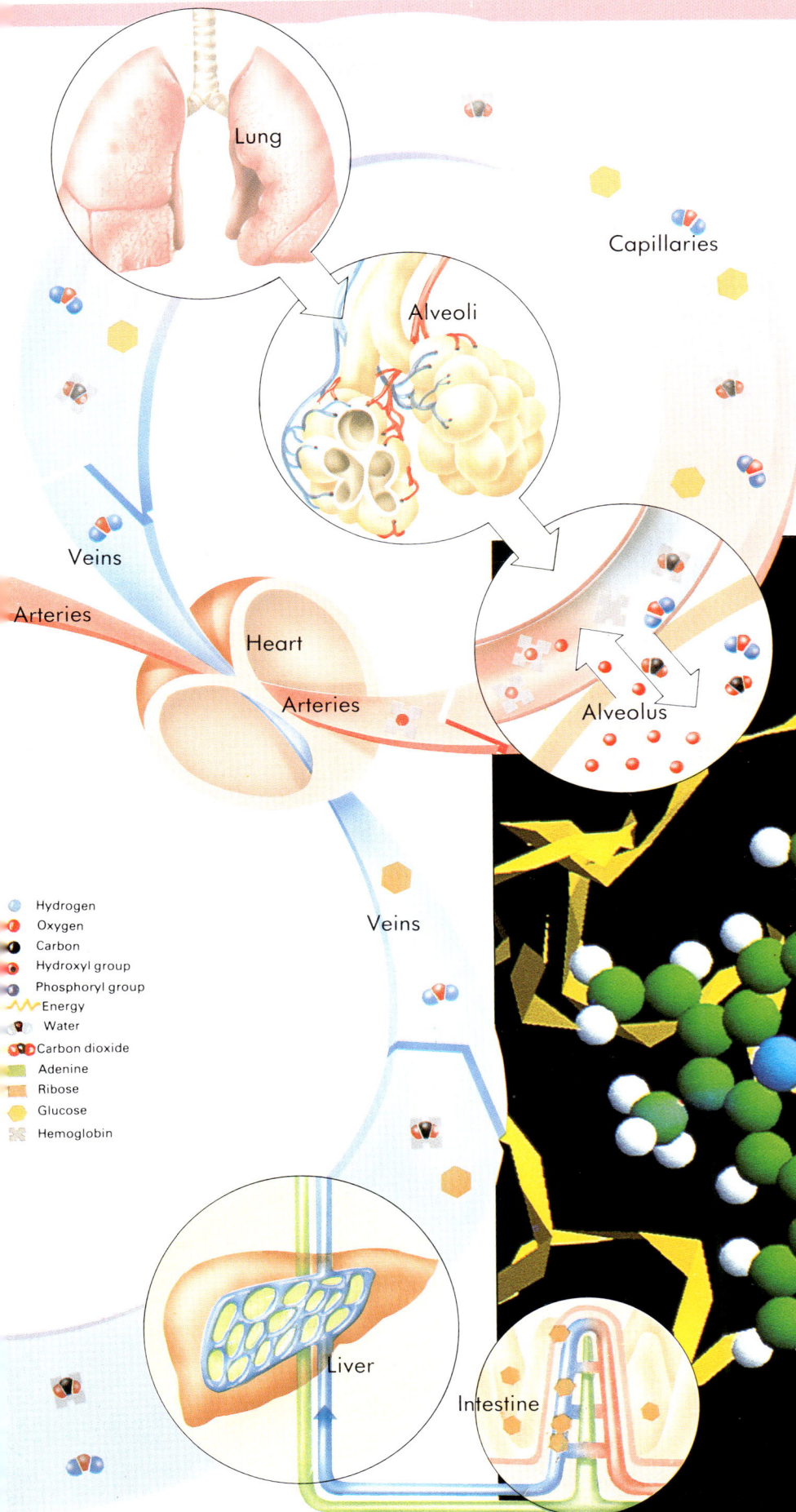

◄▼ Molecules of oxygen from the air we breathe pass through the walls of the alveoli into the blood where they combine with haemoglobin. At the same time the waste products of respiration – carbon dioxide and water – leave the blood and enter the alveoli, where they are ready to be breathed out. Glucose provides the fuel for the body's activities. It is taken into the bloodstream from carbohydrates in the food, in the intestine. It goes to the liver where it may be released into the bloodstream or stored. The haemoglobin molecule (photo below) has a unique structure with an iron atom (purple) at its centre which attracts oxygen.

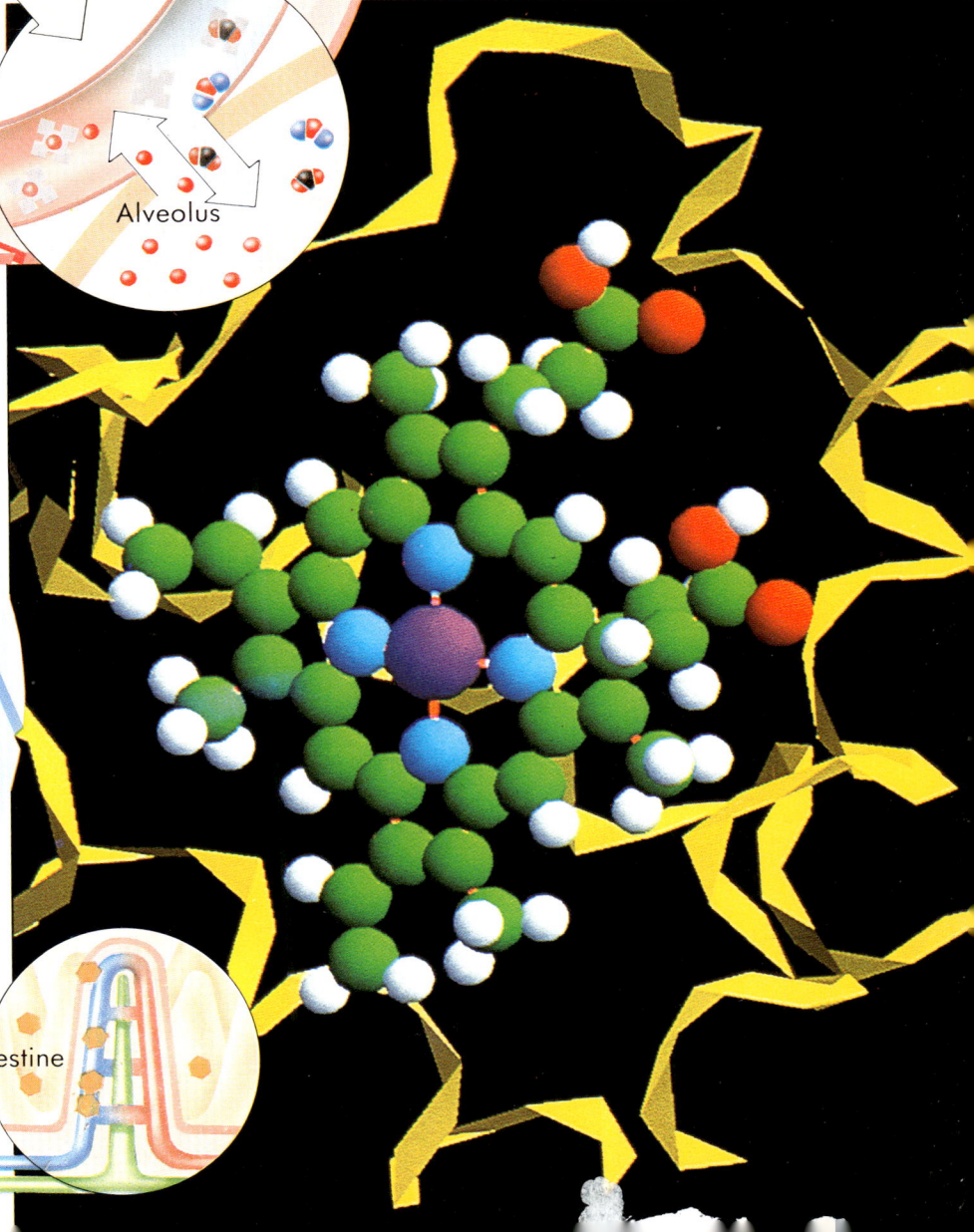

Veins

Liver

Intestine

Digestion and excretion

Spot facts

● *Children need about 4 g of body-building protein per day for each kilogram of their weight.*

● *The human liver is involved in more than 500 of the body's chemical processes.*

● *A kidney processes nearly 2,000 litres of blood every day.*

● *It can take more than a day for food to pass through the digestive system.*

● *In an adult the total length of the digestive system may be as much as 9 m.*

The food you eat provides your body with the fuel it needs to keep going and with the nutrients it must have for growth and repairs.

Some of the food you have eaten recently has become part of you, perhaps part of a muscle or your skin, while much of it has been used to give you energy to stay alive and keep moving. The remaining food was not used and has passed out of your body as waste.

Your digestive system has the task of breaking down all the things that you eat into smaller and smaller fragments. The smallest of these fragments are the molecules that your cells can use. Your liver and kidneys are part of this process. The liver controls how some of these substances from digestion are used; it stores some of them, and with the kidneys, disposes of the rest.

▶ A baby's first teeth emerge at about seven months. After that, the "milk teeth" are produced at about one a month until there is a full set of 20: eight incisors, four canines and eight molars. At the age of about six, the first of the 32 adult teeth appear and one by one push the milk teeth out.

Teeth

Before the nutrients from your food can be absorbed into the bloodstream and taken to your body cells the food must be broken down both physically and chemically. This process is called digestion and begins at the moment you put food into your mouth.

Teeth are used to cut and grind food as you chew. Small pieces of food form a pulp which is rolled into a ball by the tongue and mixed with a watery digestive fluid called saliva. Saliva is produced by salivary glands in the cheeks and under the tongue. It contains the first of a series of digestive enzymes which begin to break down the starch in food.

Babies are usually born without teeth. During their first two years of life, as they change from an all-milk diet to one which contains solid foods, they grow a set of 20 "milk teeth". At the age of about 6 years, a child's milk teeth are replaced by permanent adult teeth. A full set of adult teeth numbers 32, although some people never develop their four back molars, the wisdom teeth.

Only the upper part of a tooth, the crown, is visible above the gums. Most of the tooth is root and is concealed below the surface. The root may be three times as long as the crown. The root is anchored firmly in the jawbone and holds the tooth in place. A layer of tough, white enamel covers the crown. Enamel is the hardest substance found in the body and it gives teeth the strength they need to chew the hardest foods. Beneath the enamel is a softer bone-like substance known as dentine. In the centre of the dentine, each tooth has a cavity that contains blood vessels and nerves.

Tooth enamel is tough enough to stand up to most foods but it is easily attacked by the acids produced by some bacteria. These bacteria live on dirty teeth and feed on the sugar in sweet foods. As they do so they form the acid which may soften enamel. Enamel has no nerves and a person may be unaware of the damage. The pain of a toothache only occurs when food or drink penetrates the enamel to the dentine and the sensitive nerves inside.

One way of strengthening tooth enamel against decay is the use of the chemical fluoride. Over the last twenty years fluoride has been used in toothpastes and in some places it has been added to water supplies. This, and improved dental care, has reduced the amount of tooth decay in the developed world by half over the last twenty-five years.

Inside a tooth

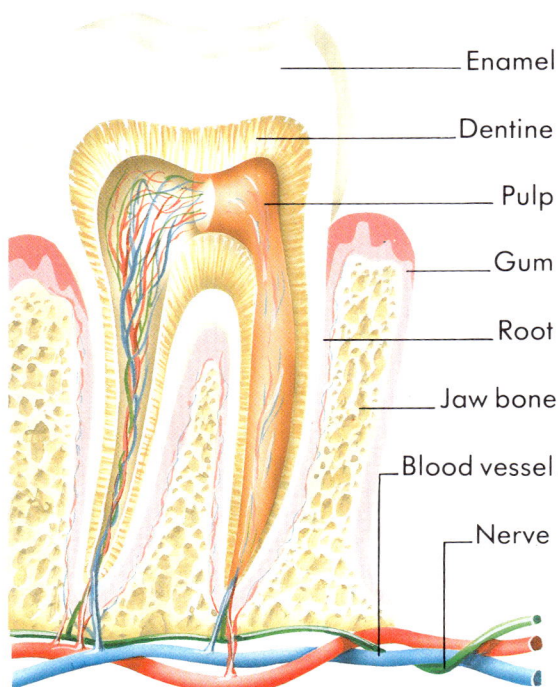

Enamel

Dentine

Pulp

Gum

Root

Jaw bone

Blood vessel

Nerve

◀ The root of a molar tooth is surrounded by hard cement which binds it firmly in place in the jawbone. Above the gum, the soft dentine around the pulp cavity is covered by hard enamel. Enamel is made mostly of calcium carbonate and calcium phosphate, whereas dentine is similar to bone.

▶ A full set of adult teeth contains 32 teeth. There are 8 flat incisors at the front for cutting food, 4 pointed canine teeth at the side for tearing and 20 pre-molars and molars at the rear of the mouth with uneven surfaces that grind and crush food.

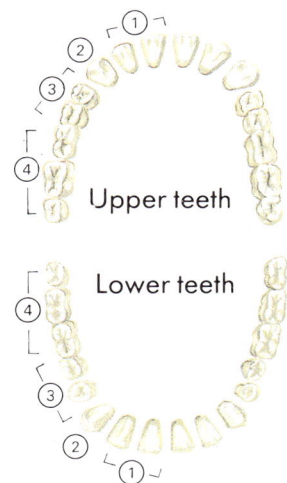

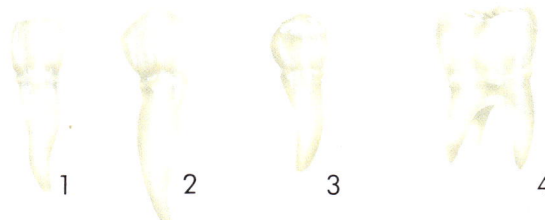

Upper teeth

Lower teeth

1

2

3

4

Key
1 Incisors
2 Canines
3 Pre-molars
4 Molars

The digestive system

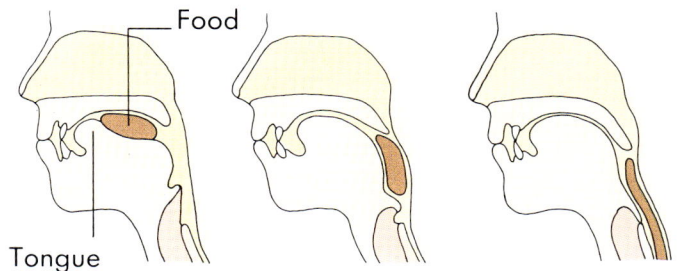

The digestive system

Salivary glands

Oesophagus

Liver

Stomach

Small intestine

Large intestine

Anus

Food

Tongue

▲ Food is swallowed as the tongue forces it to the back of the throat. The muscles at the top of the oesophagus open and food passes down to the stomach, pushed along by waves of muscle movement.

Once food has been chewed in the mouth it is swallowed and travels through the digestive system. This journey can take over 24 hours.

Food is squeezed along the digestive system rather like toothpaste along a tube. Muscles in the walls of the digestive tube contract in waves of movement called peristalsis and push food on its way.

Food stays in the stomach for about three hours. It is turned over and over by contractions of the stomach muscles and mixed with gastric juices produced by the stomach walls. It leaves the stomach as a creamy soup known as chyme.

A little at a time, chyme is passed into the small intestine. Here it is mixed with enzymes produced by the intestine walls and the pancreas. Eventually digestion is complete and nutrients are able to pass through the intestine walls. The 6 m of small intestine that are packed into the body provide an enormous surface area where absorption can take place into the bloodstream.

Undigested food passes on into the large intestine. Here some water is absorbed back into the body and the remaining waste, now called faeces, moves on into the last section of the intestine, the rectum. It can be stored here for a short while before it leaves the body through the anus. An average of 80-180 g of faeces is excreted daily.

◀ The digestive system begins at the mouth and ends at the anus. Its total length is 8-9 m. The narrowest part of the system is the oesophagus and the widest is the stomach which can stretch to take a whole meal. Most of the digestive process takes place in the small intestine, which has a large surface area and is well supplied with blood vessels to absorb the nutrients.

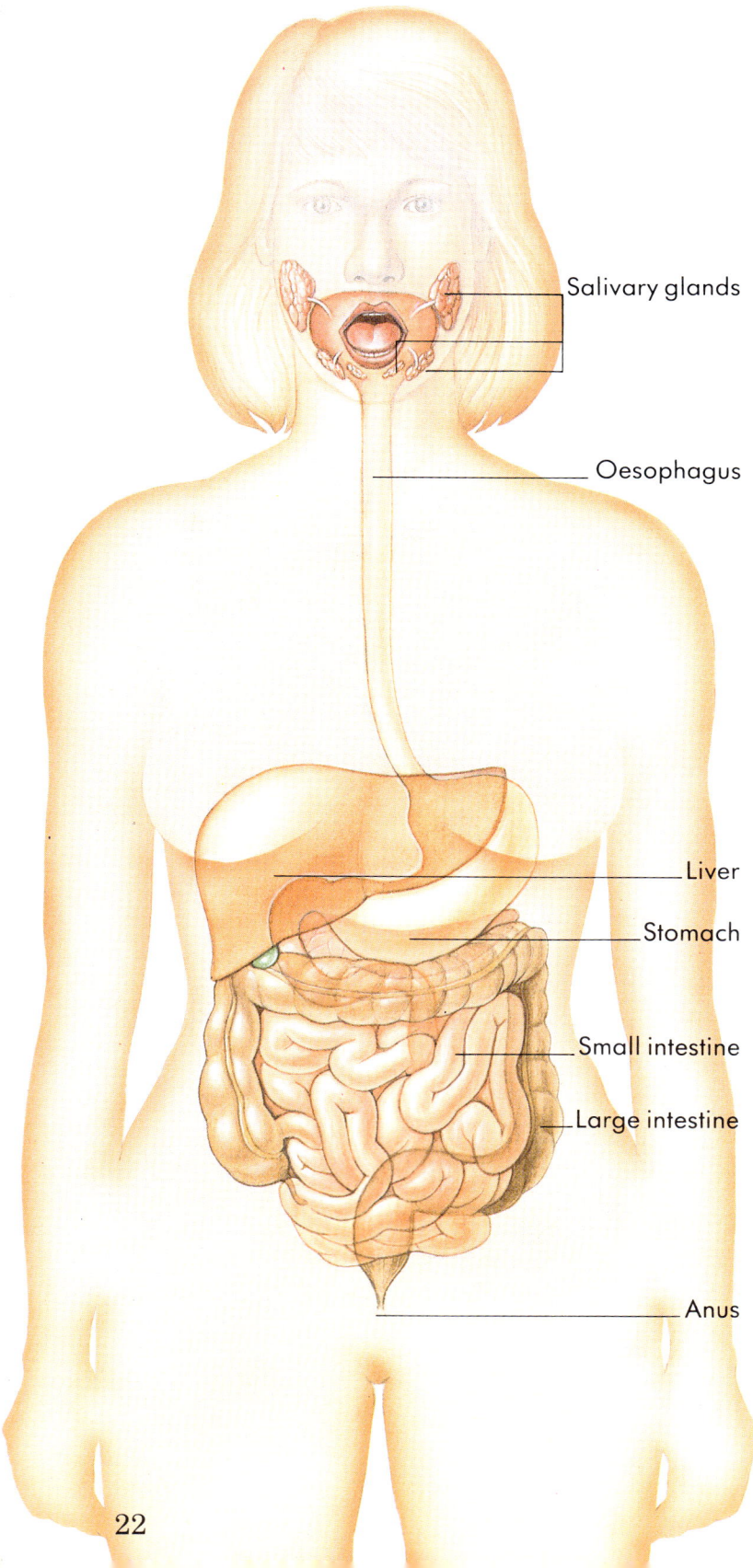

How food is broken down

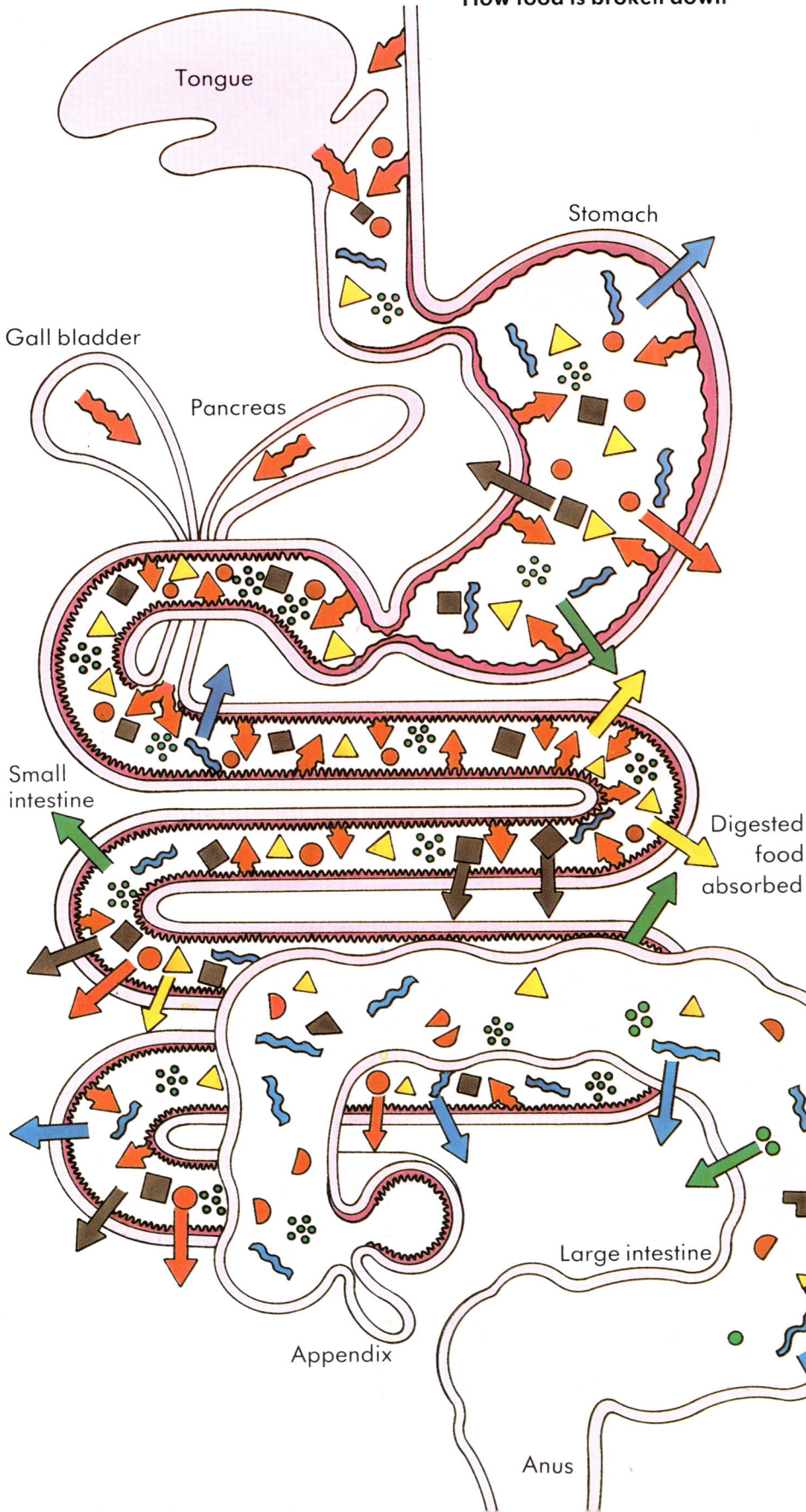

◀ Water, salts, glucose and vitamins can be absorbed directly into the bloodstream. But most foods are carbohydrates, proteins and fats which have large, complicated molecules. These must be broken down into small, simple substances before they can pass through the intestine walls. Only then can they be absorbed by the blood so that the body cells can make use of them.

Once the teeth have chopped up the food, enzymes in the digestive system act on it to complete the chemical process of digestion.

Enzymes are found in saliva in the mouth and in gastric juices produced by the stomach walls. However, most proteins and almost all fats are broken down by enzymes that are mixed with food in the small intestine. Some of these enzymes are produced by the intestine walls and others are added from the pancreas. Pancreatic juice contains the only enzymes that can digest fats and the liver produces bile which activates them.

The lining of the small intestine is creased into tiny folds that increase its total area to about 20 sq m. Each individual fold has its own supply of blood capillaries, which carry away digested protein and carbohydrates. The folds in the small intestine are also supplied with lymph vessels which absorb digested fat.

Tongue

Stomach

Gall bladder

Pancreas

Small intestine

Digested food absorbed

Large intestine

Appendix

Anus

△ Protein

■ Fats

● Carbohydrate

Vitamins Minerals

Water

Enzymes

The liver

The liver weighs more than 1½ kg. It is the body's largest and most complicated organ, and is shaped like a pyramid. It is very complex. It takes part in several hundred chemical reactions that control the composition of the blood and supply the needs of other organs.

One of its most important jobs is to process the nutrients that are absorbed from the intestine. The liver regulates the amounts of vitamins and energy-giving sugars in the blood by storing them when they are plentiful. It also converts unwanted protein into urea, a substance that is disposed of by the kidneys. Surplus sugar is converted into glycogen which is stored when the level of sugar in the blood is high, but can be released rapidly if the level falls.

The liver also acts as a recycling plant. It breaks down old red blood cells and extracts the haemoglobin from them. Some of the substances this process produces can be reused but some cannot. These wastes are taken to the gall bladder and disposed of in bile. The liver acts on substances such as alcohol and drugs which would poison the body if they were not treated. It also makes some blood-clotting factors.

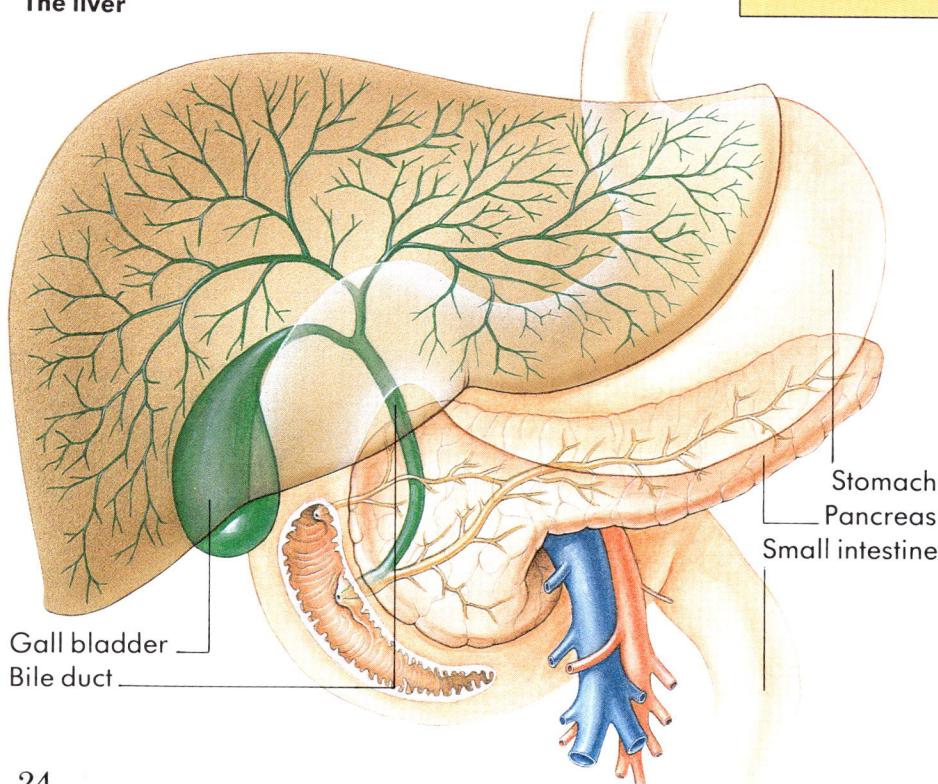

Hepatic vein
Liver
Heart
Hepatic artery
Hepatic portal vein
Stomach
Small intestine

The liver receives about one fifth of its blood oxygen-rich from the heart. The remainder comes from the small intestine via the hepatic portal vein. The blood enters a capillary network once it is inside the liver.

The liver

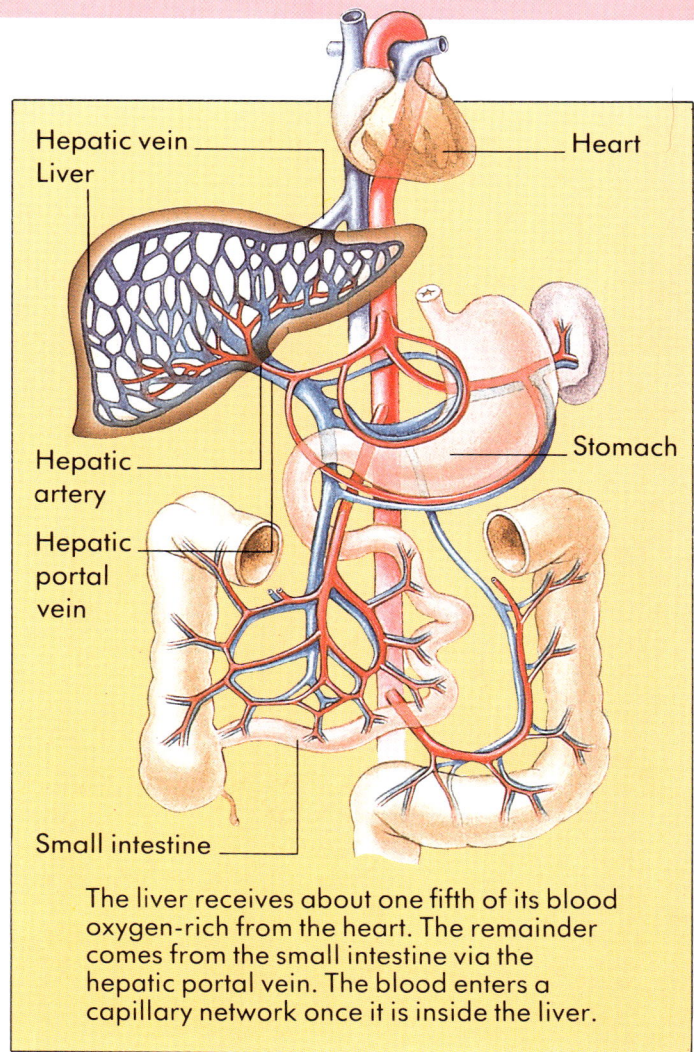

Gall bladder
Bile duct
Stomach
Pancreas
Small intestine

◄ The liver produces as much as 1 litre of bile each day. Bile is stored in a small bag called the gall bladder which is found just below the liver. It passes into the small intestine along the bile duct. Bile is a greenish colour and contains bilirubin, a waste product from the breakdown of haemoglobin.

Lying close to the liver is the pancreas, which produces digestive enzymes and also makes insulin. Insulin controls the amount of glycogen stored by the liver.

The kidneys

The kidneys have two important functions. One is to regulate the amount of water and salts in the body so that cells are able to continue their chemical reactions. The second is to dispose of waste protein, in the form of the urea.

Each kidney is made of more than a million tiny tubules called nephrons. Nephrons are minute filtering units. At the end of each nephron a capsule surrounds a knot of blood capillaries. Blood plasma containing water, salts, and other chemicals, filters through the capsule and passes along the nephron.

Most of the water and substances such as glucose, which the body needs, are reabsorbed into the bloodstream. However, waste substances from the liver and other organs remain inside the tubules together with water and salts that are not required.

The liquid that flows from the nephrons down to the bladder is called urine. About 1 litre of urine is produced each day. In hot weather when water is lost through sweating this amount will be much lower as the kidneys absorb back more water to maintain the correct level in the body.

The kidneys

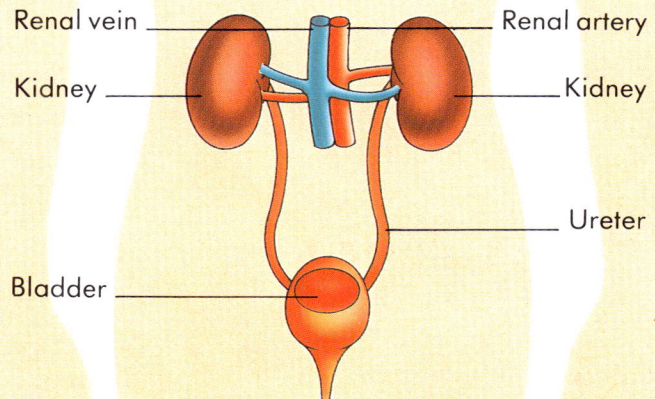

Renal vein — Renal artery
Kidney — Kidney
Ureter
Bladder

The kidneys are situated just below the ribs at the back of the body. Each kidney receives blood from the renal artery. The ureters carry urine from the kidneys down to the bladder which can hold up to 600 ml of urine. Blood leaves the kidneys through the renal vein.

Inside the kidney

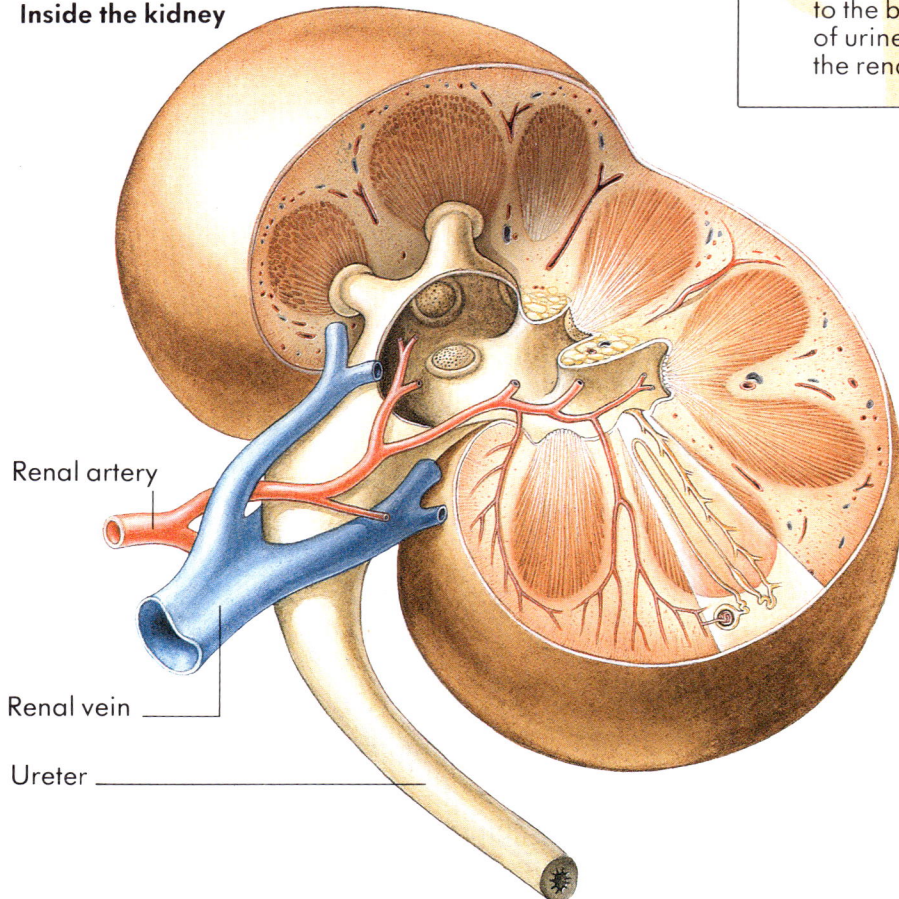

Renal artery
Renal vein
Ureter

◀ Each kidney is about 100 mm long and 50 mm wide. Inside the kidney there are three main regions. Branches of the renal artery go to the outer layer, the cortex, which contains the cup-shaped openings to the kidney tubules. The tubules loop into the medulla and back into the cortex before they join up together, finally ending at the centre of the kidney. Here, urine flows out of the tubules into the end of the ureter, and from there to the bladder.

Controlling the body

● The brain is thought to contain 25,000 million individual nerve cells.

● The fastest nerves can transmit messages at over 120 m per second.

● The longest nerve fibres are about 1 m long. They stretch from the base of the spinal cord to the tip of the foot.

● The pituitary gland, situated in the middle of the brain, is often called the "master gland" because it controls the work of the other glands.

● The pituitary gland is only 1.3 cm across.

● One form of diabetes, diabetes mellitus, is the most common defect of the hormone system.

► This man covered with needles seems to feel no pain. The brain normally receives messages of pain from nerve endings. In some conditions the brain appears able to prevent sensations of pain from reaching it. Another method the brain has of dealing with severe pain is to release a chemical called an endomorphin, which suppresses pain sensations.

All the processes that go on inside your body, as well as your thoughts, emotions and memories, must be well organized and coordinated. It is the brain at the centre of the control system that keeps everything in the body running smoothly. The brain receives information about what is happening both inside your body and in the world. The information being gathered all the time by your senses is sent speeding to the brain through a network of nerves. Acting on the information it receives, your brain automatically controls some activities such as breathing and heartbeat. Other activities require you to think before you decide what to do.

The nervous system

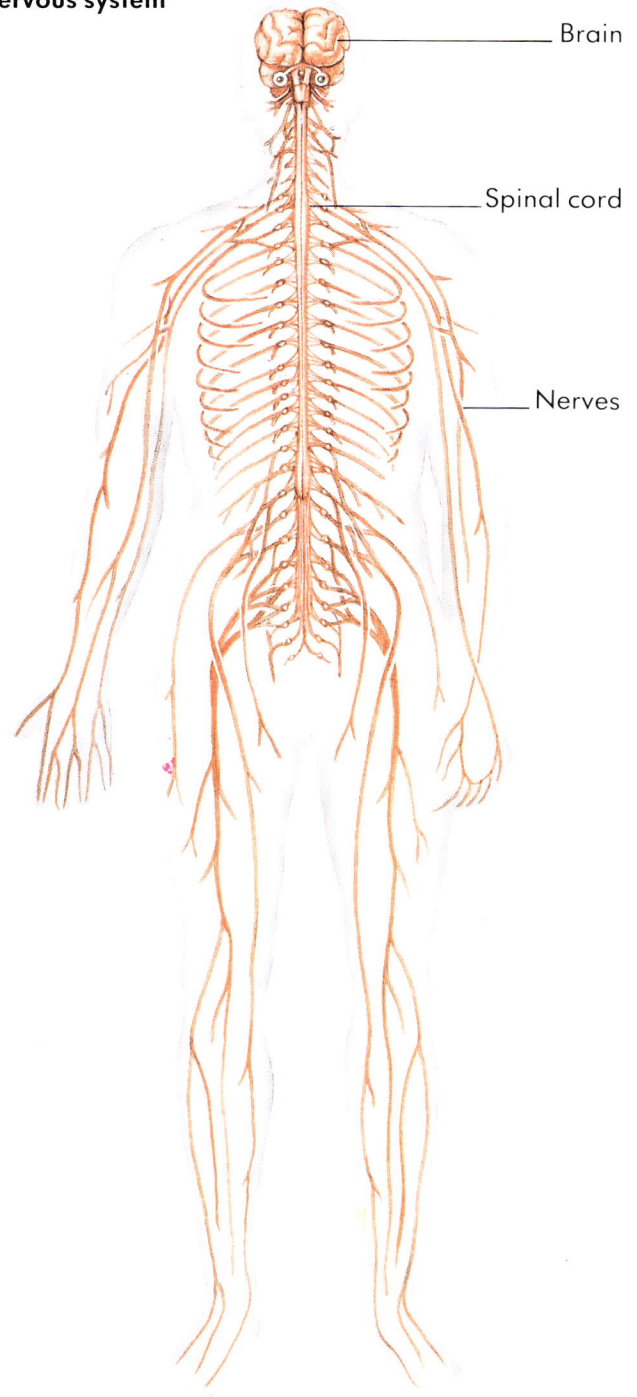

The nervous system is the control and communication system that ensures all the different parts of the body work in harmony. The brain and spinal cord make up the central part of the system and receive messages from a network of nerves.

Most of the cells which make up the nervous system are neurones. These cells have the ability to carry and transmit the tiny electrical impulses that make up a nerve message. There are sensory neurones which carry impulses to the brain, and motor neurones which carry them away. Each neurone has a cell body with a number of fine fibres branching from it. Most have several short fibres known as dendrites, and just one long fibre called an axon. The axon carries messages from the cell body to be passed on to the dendrites of the next cell.

The ends of axons and dendrites do not touch one another. As an impulse reaches the end of one axon it has to cross a gap to reach the next cell. As messages arrive, a chemical called a neuro-transmitter is released. This chemical's job is to bridge the gap for an instant until the message has passed.

The nervous system

Brain

Spinal cord

Nerves

A nerve cell

Extending from the body of this nerve cell is a long axon, covered with an insulating layer of a fatty substance called myelin. Myelin helps the transmission of impulses.

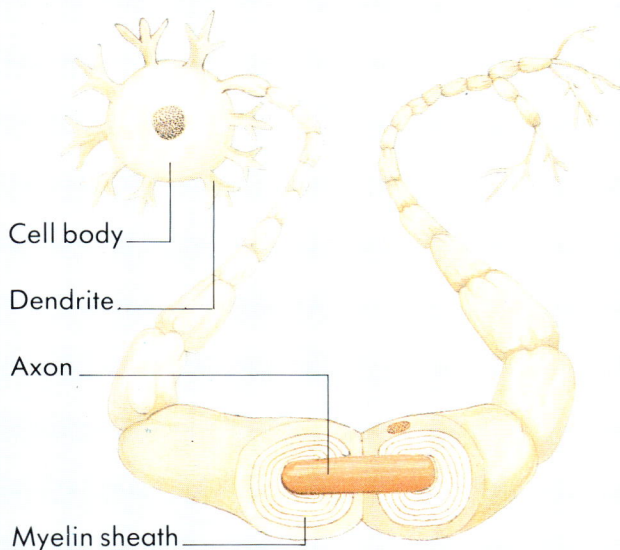

Cell body

Dendrite

Axon

Myelin sheath

▲ The central nervous system consists of the brain and spinal cord. The peripheral nervous system is made up of the cranial nerves which branch from the brain and the spinal nerves which branch from the spinal cord. There are 31 pairs of spinal nerves; 8 go to the neck, shoulders and arms, 12 to the chest, 5 pairs control the legs and feet and the remainder control the pelvic organs and buttocks.

Sensing surroundings

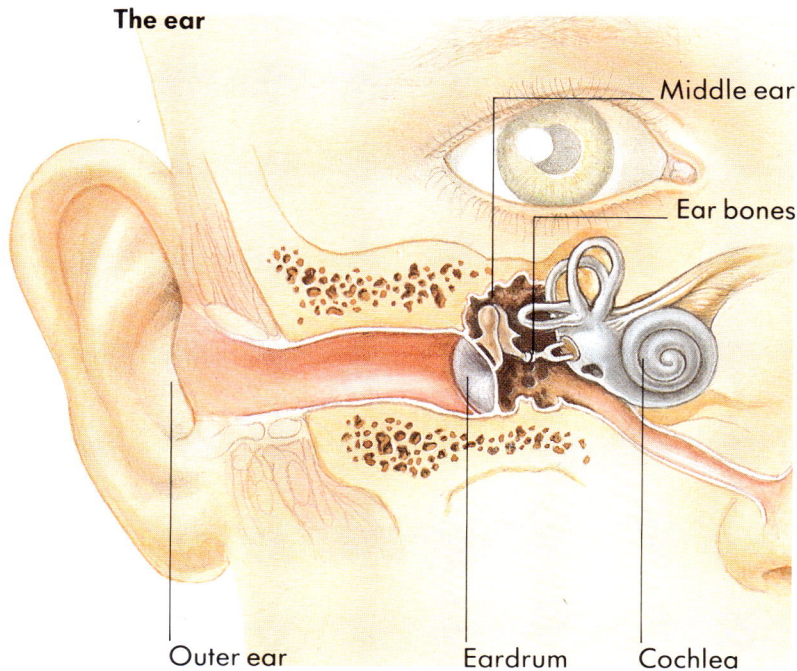

The ear

Middle ear

Ear bones

Outer ear   Eardrum   Cochlea

We rely on our five senses – sight, hearing, smell, taste and touch – to supply information about the world around us. Our sense organs are only detectors: the brain interprets the information they collect.

The ear detects the vibrations of the air that form sounds. Vibrations are directed through the ear to a fluid-filled inner chamber, called the cochlea. The fluid inside this structure takes up the vibrations, disturbing thousands of sensitive hairs as it does so. Cells attached to the hairs send nerve impulses to the brain, where the vibrations are decoded into sounds.

Sight is so important that 80 per cent of what the brain knows has come from the eyes. The retina lining the inside of the eyeball is made up of two kinds of light-sensitive cells, called rods and cones. Rods work in dim light and detect black and white; cones detect colour and work only in bright light.

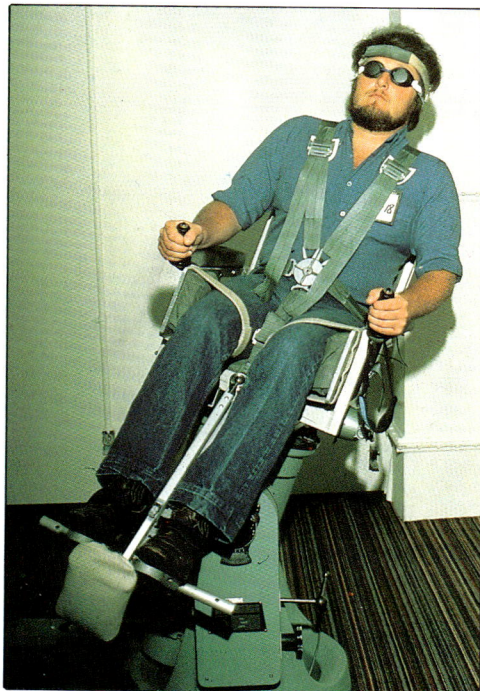

◀▲ The outer ear collects sound waves. The middle ear then transmits them to the inner ear, which passes the messages to the brain.

Pupil

Lens

Iris

Nerve to brain

Cornea

Retina

Image

Object

Cornea

Lens

Retina

▲ This strange device is testing the sense of balance of a trainee astronaut. Balance receptors are three semi-circular canals in the inner part of the ear. Each canal is filled with fluid and arranged at right angles to the others. Movement in any direction disturbs the fluid and sensitive nerves in the canal. The brain combines information from all three canals to give us a sense of position and rotation.

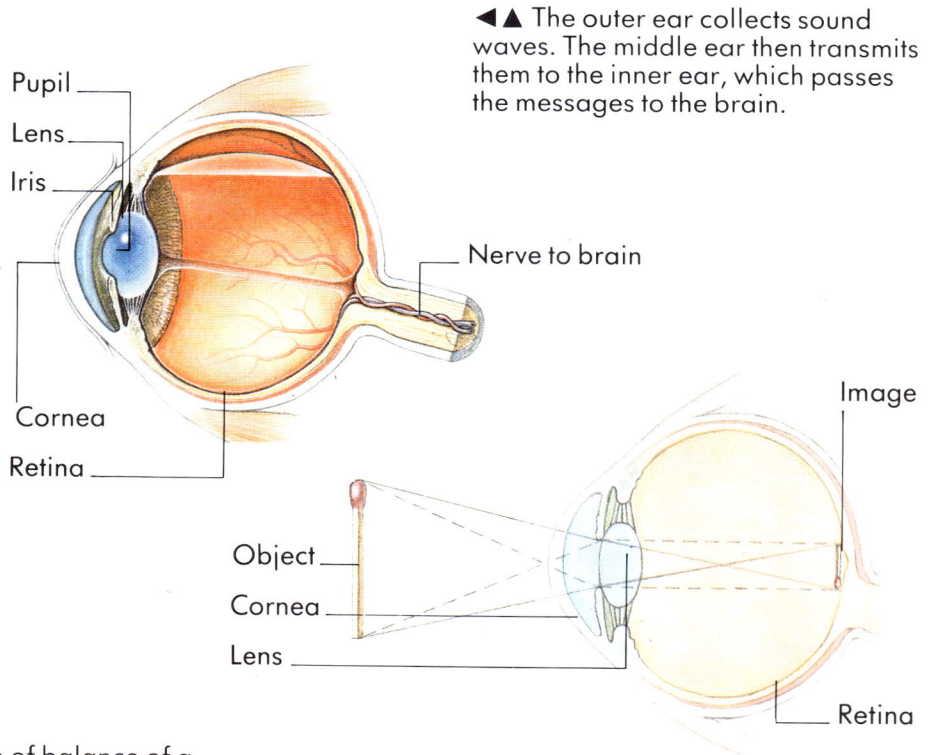

▲ Rays of light from objects enter the eye through the pupil. They are focused by the cornea and the lens, and an upside-down image falls on the retina. Messages travel to the brain along the optic nerve.

Taste and smell sensors are both stimulated by chemicals. Smell receptors cover an area the size of a postage stamp in the upper part of the nose. They respond to tiny molecules of scent in the air. If you need to identify a particular smell, a sniff will carry as many scent molecules as possible to the receptors.

Tastes are distinguished by small groups of receptors in the taste buds on the tongue. Taste buds are not evenly distributed on the tongue, and some parts are more sensitive than others. There are distinct receptors for sweet, sour, salty and bitter tastes.

Even without our other senses, we can still learn a lot about our surroundings from our sense of touch. Thousands of receptors in the skin enable us to detect different temperatures, textures and pressures, and to feel pain. Pain receptors are the most numerous because pain warns the body that something is wrong.

Taste and smell

Scent receptors

Nasal cavity

Taste receptors

Tongue

▼ This woman is reading braille with her fingertips. Touch receptors allow her to identify the raised dots which form letters and words. An experienced reader can "read" up to 50 words per minute.

▲ Taste receptors are found only on the tongue and smell receptors only in the nasal cavity. The senses are quite separate but they work closely together. When you have a cold and cannot smell, you taste less accurately.

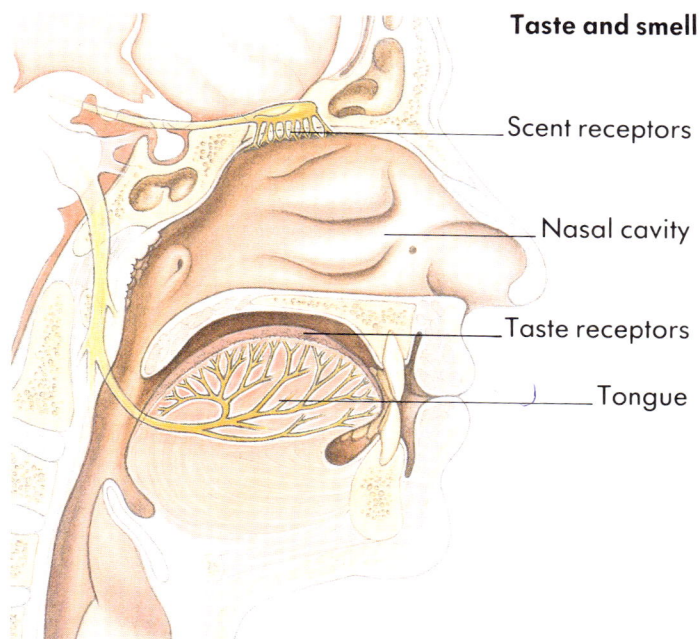

The tongue

Sweet

Salty

Sour

Bitter

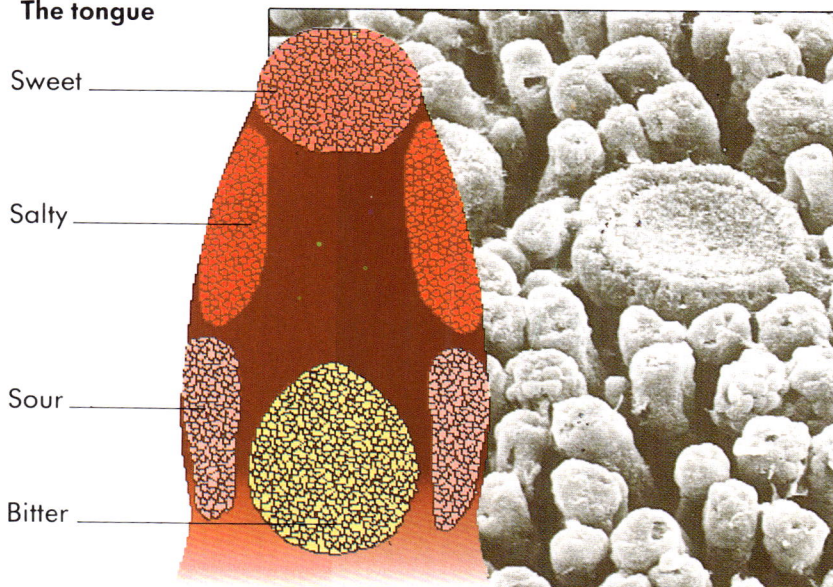

▲ A human tongue is about 10 cm long and has about 9,000 taste buds. Some parts of the tongue are more sensitive to certain tastes than others. The front of the tongue detects sweet tastes, while the sides respond to salty and sour food. The enlarged photograph on the right shows the large taste buds found at the back of the mouth. These detect bitter tastes.

Inside the brain

The brain is the largest and most complicated part of the nervous system. It is shielded by the skull and surrounded by protective membranes and fluid. The brain weighs about 1.3 kg, only about 2 per cent of the body's weight, and yet it uses about 20 per cent of the body's energy.

The brain has three main parts, the brain stem, the cerebellum and the cerebrum. Each part has a different job to do. The brain stem is connected to the spinal cord. It contains groups of neurones that control involuntary activities such as digestion, breathing and the circulation of blood. The cerebellum coordinates our muscles so that our movements are smooth and we stay evenly balanced. It is situated at the back of the head.

The cerebrum is the largest part of the brain. It is responsible for all our thoughts and voluntary actions. The cerebrum is divided into two large sections called hemispheres which are linked by bands of nerves. In general, the left hemisphere controls the activities of the right hand side of the body and vice versa.

The folded outer layers of the cerebrum are known as the cortex. The cortex forms a layer of "grey matter" covering an area of more than 2,500 sq cm over the two hemispheres. The cortex receives all your conscious sensations and it stops and starts all your voluntary movements. It is responsible for your judgement and some of your emotions and it is the part of the brain that allows you to learn.

Different parts of the cortex handle information coming from different receptors in the body. They are known as sensory areas. There is one which deals with messages from the ears, another with visual information and so on. Once the information has been processed it can be used for making decisions. The brain must tell the body what to do and these instructions are sent from a special motor area of the cortex.

▼ The largest part of the human brain is the cerebrum, with its folded outer layer the cortex. The two halves of the cerebrum are linked by more than 100 million nerve fibres which form the *corpus callosum*. The optic and olfactory nerves carry messages directly to the brain.

The brain

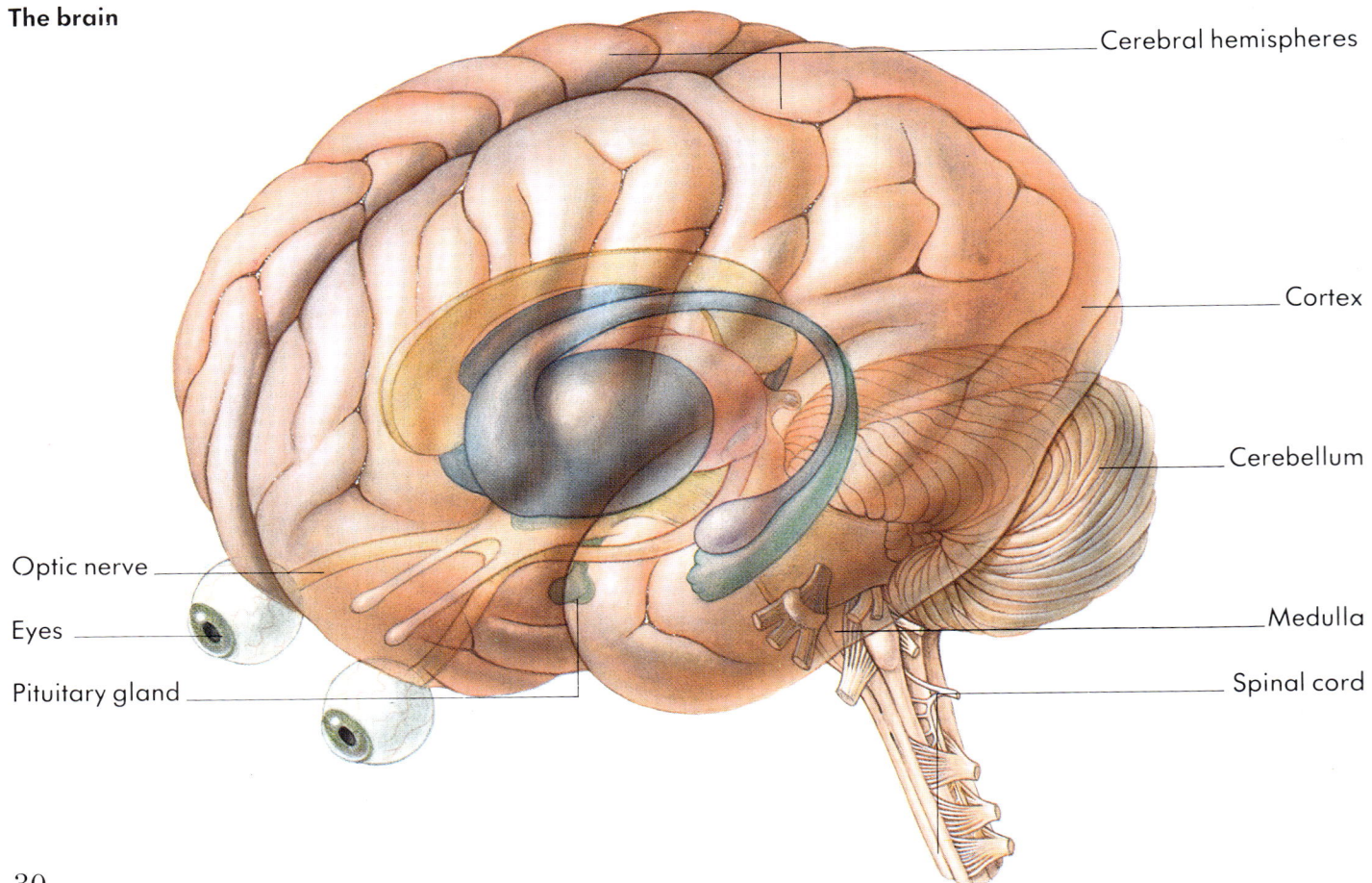

Cerebral hemispheres

Cortex

Cerebellum

Optic nerve

Eyes

Pituitary gland

Medulla

Spinal cord

The control of many body activities is not shared equally between the two halves of the cerebrum. Right-handed people tend to use the left side of the brain to control reasoning, language and their skill at mathematics. The right side of the brain is more important for artistic qualities, such as imagination and perception of space and the interpretation of music and art. For left-handed people these activities are reversed, although the exact division varies slightly from person to person.

Beneath the cerebrum, in the centre of the brain, are the hypothalamus and the pituitary gland, often called the "master gland". Together, these two control the body over a long period of time, regulating processes such as growth and reproduction. The hypothalamus directs the pituitary gland which stimulates other glands to produce their hormones.

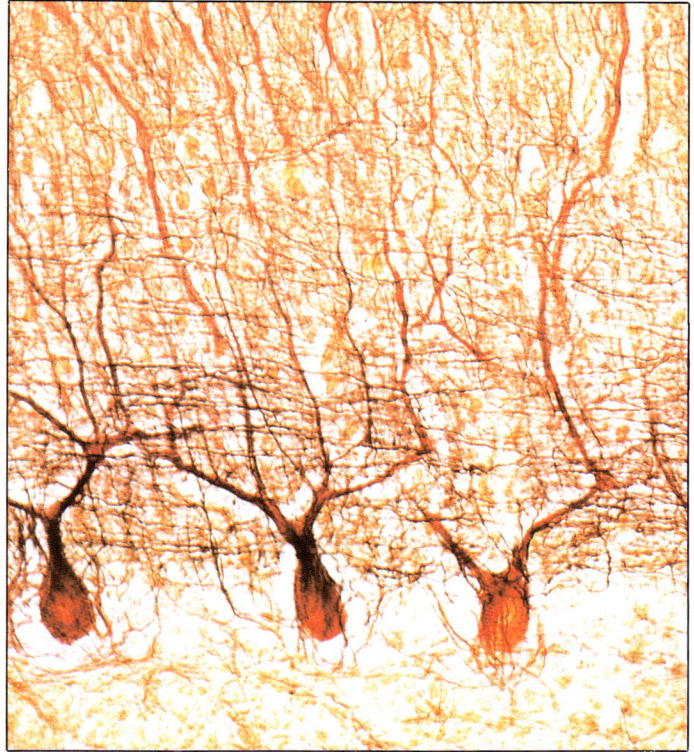

▶ The nerve cells in the cortex have many nerve fibres branching from them. This provides thousands of possibilities for different connections in the brain.

Brain sizes

Cerebrum   Medulla

1 Fish

2 Amphibian

3 Reptile

4 Bird

5 Mammal

6 Human

These diagrams show the relative sizes of the brains of various animals from fish (1), to amphibians (2), reptiles (3), birds (4), mammals (5) and humans (6). The size of the cerebellum, responsible for coordination and control, becomes progressively larger. So also does the size of the cerebrum.

Humans have a particularly large cerebrum compared with the other animals. The two hemispheres of the cerebrum account for 90 per cent of the volume of the whole brain. The average weight of a man's brain is 1,350 g and that of a woman is 1,200 g. Women have a higher ratio of brain to body weight.

Functions of the brain

Different parts of the cortex are responsible for different functions in the body. We can identify which areas are which. For example, the visual cortex, the sensory area which receives messages from the eyes, is at the back of the skull. When we sleep the entire cortex works more slowly, but if it should be damaged, it can stop working completely and cause unconsciousness. Damage to just one area can affect the control of a specific activity. This can happen in the case of a stroke, which interrupts the supply of blood to certain parts of the cortex. The cells in those parts may die. A stroke which

The cortex of the brain

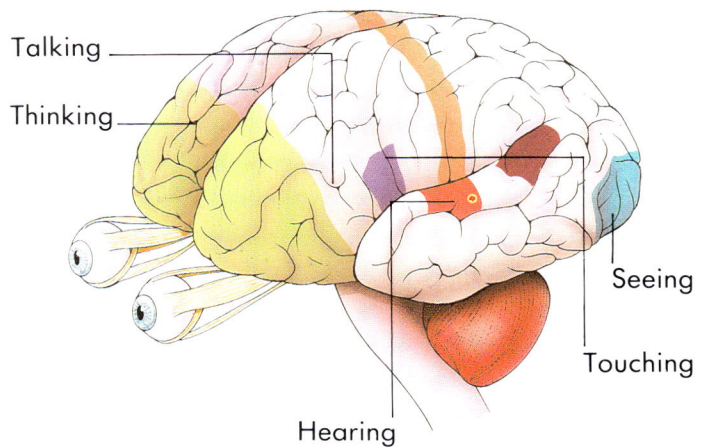

Talking
Thinking
Seeing
Touching
Hearing

▶ The different areas responsible for various body functions can be identified on a map of the cortex. Thought takes place at the front of the brain; hearing, speech and reading are coordinated at the side.

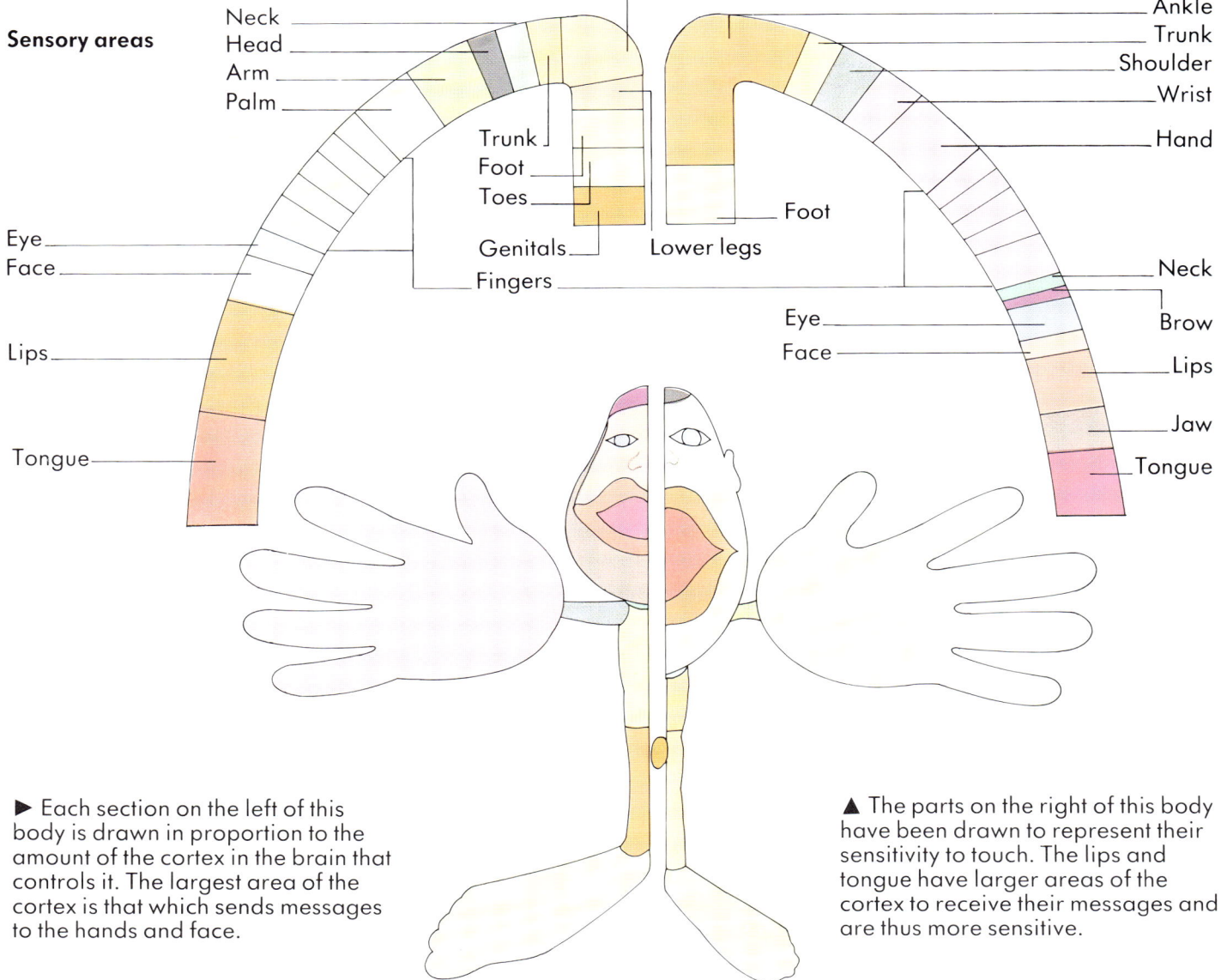

Sensory areas

Neck
Head
Arm
Palm

Trunk
Foot
Toes
Genitals
Fingers

Upper legs
Ankle
Trunk
Shoulder
Wrist
Hand

Foot
Lower legs

Eye
Face

Lips

Tongue

Eye
Face

Neck
Brow
Lips
Jaw
Tongue

▶ Each section on the left of this body is drawn in proportion to the amount of the cortex in the brain that controls it. The largest area of the cortex is that which sends messages to the hands and face.

▲ The parts on the right of this body have been drawn to represent their sensitivity to touch. The lips and tongue have larger areas of the cortex to receive their messages and are thus more sensitive.

affects the motor area of the left hemisphere can paralyse parts of the right hand side of the body and cause a loss of speech. Certain areas deep in the brain are known to store our memories but exactly how they work is not understood. It may be that if the same connections between neurones are made frequently, pathways through them may be established, and this could be the key to remembering.

There seem to be several different types of memory. "Short term" memory can last a few hours and be used to help us recall things such as telephone numbers or a shopping list. On the other hand "long term" memory can allow us to remember faces and places, and the patterns of our language and behaviour.

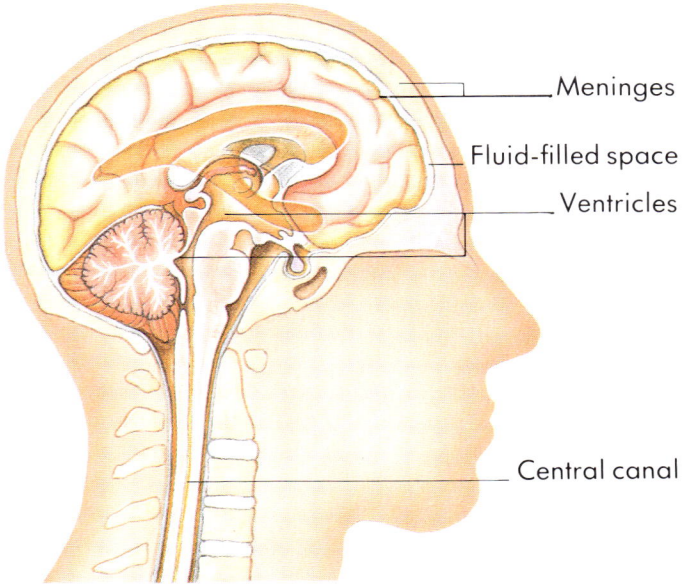

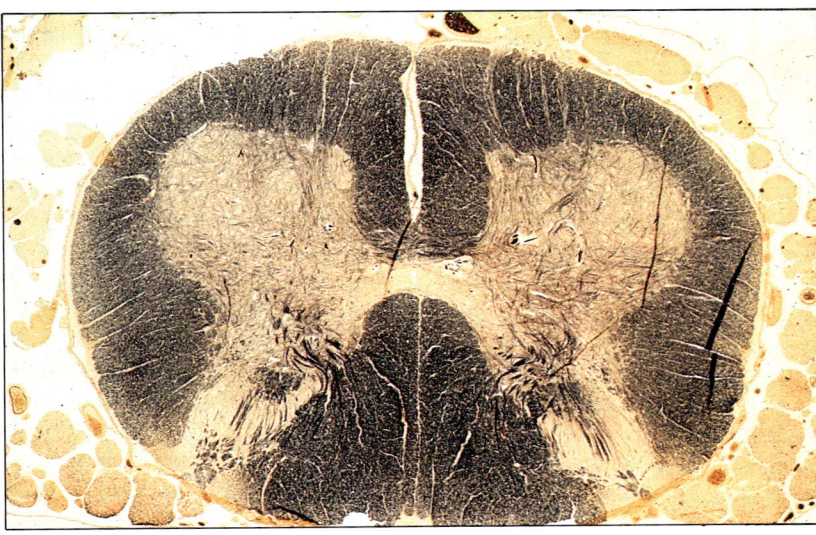

▲ Wrapped around the brain and spinal cord are two layers of protective membranes called meninges. Between them is a fluid which also fills four spaces called ventricles. The fluid acts as a cushion and prevents the delicate nerves being jolted. If bacteria or viruses get into the meninges, they may spread through the fluid and cause a serious illness called meningitis.

◄ A section through the spinal cord shows that there is an H-shaped grey area in the centre surrounded by a white area. The grey area is mainly nerve cell bodies, while the white area contains nerve fibres enclosed in their fatty, myelin coverings. The spinal cord carries information up to the brain and down and causes reflex actions.

Reflex actions

Reflex actions are automatic responses that are controlled by the spinal cord alone. Often they are used to protect the body from dangerous situations. The body relies on reflex actions when there is only one possible response and there is no time to wait for messages to be sent to and from the brain.

If, for example, you tread on a sharp nail, a sensory neurone carries a nerve impulse to the spinal cord where it connects with a motor neurone. This takes a message back to the muscle of the leg which contracts. You will automatically jerk your foot away even before a message of pain has travelled up the spinal cord to your brain.

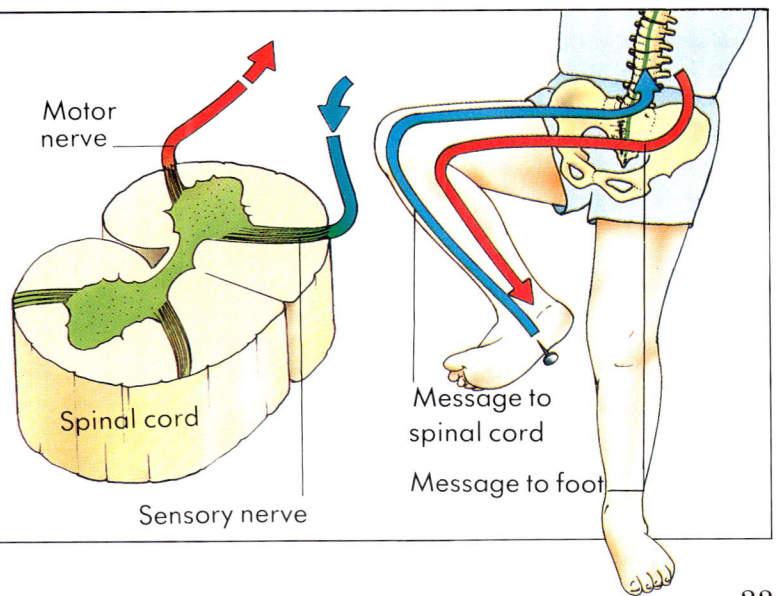

Glands and hormones

For fast responses and instant action, the body relies on its nervous system. Using electrical impulses, nerves can make muscles contract and changes happen quickly. For longer-term changes, such as growth or control of the reproductive process, the body uses a system of chemical messengers which have more lasting effects. The chemical messengers are our hormones. They are secreted directly into the bloodstream which carries them around the body. As a result, hormone messages take a little longer to travel than nerve messages. Some hormones affect the work of only one organ, while others may affect the whole body.

Hormones are made in the endocrine glands and each hormone controls a specific body process. The thyroid in the neck produces a hormone called thyroxine which regulates the

▼ The main endocrine glands are the pituitary, thyroid, parathyroid, the adrenals, the pancreas and the reproductive glands. (Although both testes and ovaries are shown on this diagram, they would not both be present in the same body.) Hormones enable the body to cope with heat, cold, stress and starvation. They control reproduction, pregnancy and birth as well as growth and development.

The hormone-producing glands

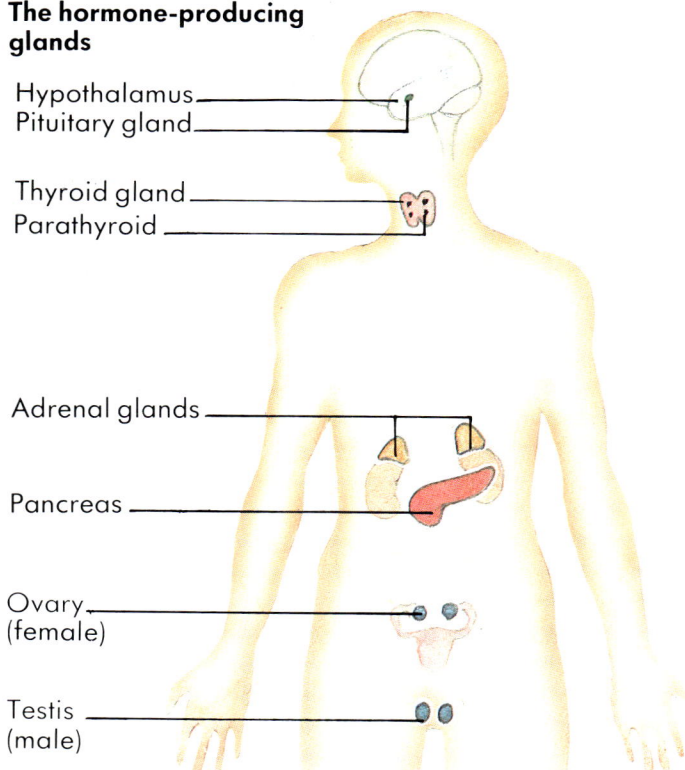

Hypothalamus
Pituitary gland

Thyroid gland
Parathyroid

Adrenal glands

Pancreas

Ovary
(female)

Testis
(male)

way the body's cells use energy. Close to it, the parathyroid produces hormones that control the way the body uses the mineral calcium. Without this hormone, bones can become weakened as the amount of calcium stored in them is reduced.

The pancreas makes the hormone insulin which also affects the body's energy use by controlling the amount of sugar in the blood. A shortage of insulin leads to the disease called diabetes.

One unusual gland is the thymus in the chest. It is present in children but shrinks and disappears in adults. It is thought that it helps the body to fight infections.

The master gland

The pituitary gland is attached to the underside of the brain. Its activities are controlled by the hypothalamus, a small region at the base of the brain, which passes messages from the nervous system. As well as producing its own hormones, the pituitary gland makes the trophic hormones which control all other glands. As a result it is often called the master gland.

The pituitary produces hormones which control the kidneys and maintain the correct level of water in the body. It also makes growth hormone, which is produced throughout childhood to control the rate at which we grow. Growth hormone is released in especially large amounts in puberty. During this period it stimulates the reproductive glands, the ovaries and the testes, to produce sex hormones. These hormones prepare the body for reproduction, as boys become men and girls become women.

Emergency service

Adrenaline is a hormone which comes from the adrenal glands, and it is unusual. It has the ability to make the body respond instantly. The adrenal glands produce two hormones, noradrenaline and adrenaline. Noradrenaline is used to keep the blood pressure constant but adrenaline acts in emergencies. When the body is calm, slightly more noradrenaline than adrenaline is produced, but in an emergency far more adrenaline is released. The effect of adrenaline is the so-called "fight or flight" response.

The "fight or flight" response

In a desperate situation you may decide to stay and fight or run away in fright. Your brain sends a message to the pituitary gland, which stimulates the adrenal gland to release adrenaline. This causes various changes. Your pupils dilate; your heart beats faster and your lungs take in more oxygen. More energy-giving sugars flow into the blood from the liver. The blood vessels in the skin become narrower. The blood supply to the muscles increases. The muscles are now ready to help you fight or run away.

The brain senses an emergency. The pituitary gland responds by stimulating the adrenal gland.

The pupils dilate.

Hairs stand on end.

Pink skin turns pale as blood vessels near the skin contract.

Muscles receive more blood, oxygen and glucose.

The lungs breathe more deeply and the breathing rate increases.

The heart dilates and beats faster.

The liver releases glucose stored for extra energy.

The adrenal gland releases adrenaline.

Digestion slows down.

Palms of the hands sweat.

Bladder control weakens.

Mind and learning

Every time we think or make a decision we are using information and ideas from our brain's store of memories. Much of what we remember, however, has to be learnt first. We begin to learn about our world from the moment we are born. Using past experiences as a guide, we learn to cope with new ones.

People learn in several different ways. The simplest is by trial and error. Very young children use this method as they pick up a series of objects to discover which one will make a noise. Adults confronted with a bunch of keys and a door will test each key in turn to discover which one fits the lock.

Later, in order to save time, the brain will use the results of previous experiences. The baby selects a rattle because he knows it makes a noise: he knows this from experience.

We learn to speak using another type of learning, imitation. Babies repeat words they hear and discover that some have useful results such as food or toys. Having learnt our own language we may attempt to learn another. To do this, imitation and practice are needed.

As we grow up, we begin to develop the ability to reason. We can analyse situations that are completely new to us. We do this in an abstract way, in our thoughts, and can predict the consequences of the actions we choose to take. This begins at about age seven.

New skills are difficult to acquire at first. A person must concentrate all their attention on the task in hand. If too many stimuli compete for the brain's attention at the same time, it has difficulty in concentrating properly on any one of them. It has difficulty learning.

► ▼ Children playing a game of chess think about the moves they are about to make and predict the consequences of what they choose to do. The ability to reason in this way does not develop until children are older. The boy (below) is using logic and experience in solving his jigsaw puzzle.

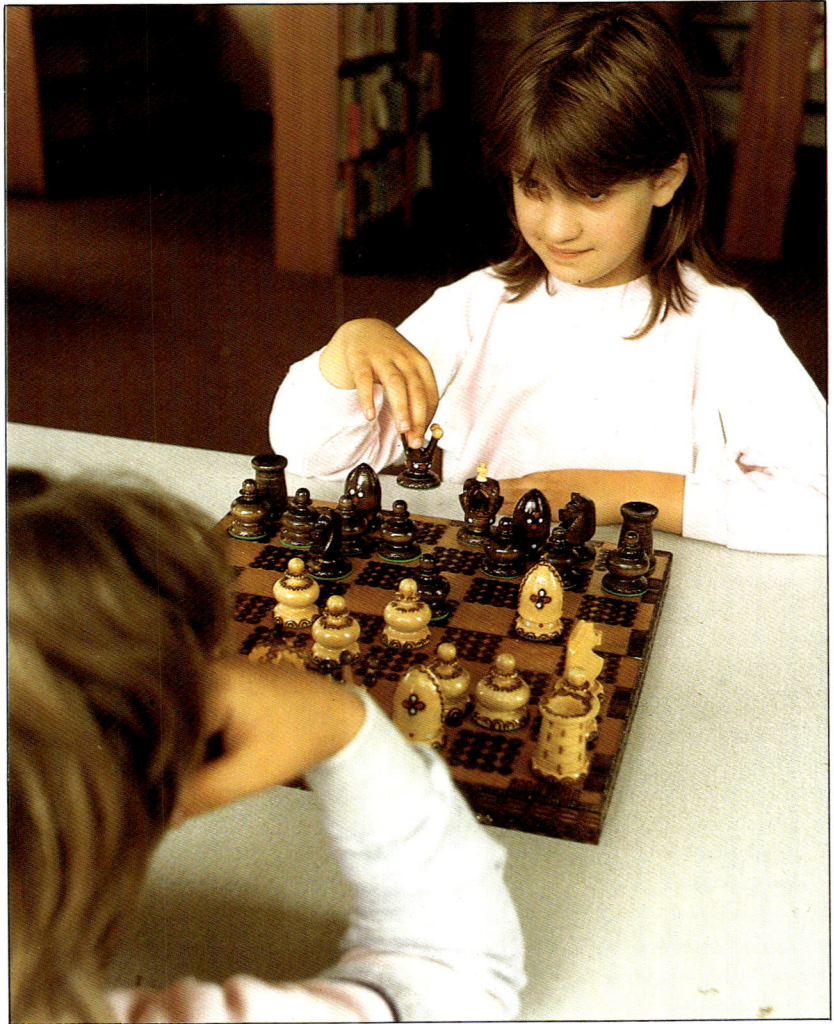

▲ These young children are trying to fit shapes into the toy cube. They are using their minds as well as their hands to match the shapes and holes.

◄ A baby will experiment with all kinds of objects to discover as much as possible about their shape, texture, and the noise they may make.

► Sign language was developed as a way of allowing deaf people to communicate. Each movement of the hands has a very precise meaning. Some TV stations have announcers "sign" the news, and other programmes, for the benefit of viewers with a hearing disability. Most of us use more general signs and gestures of the hands, eyes and head to communicate.

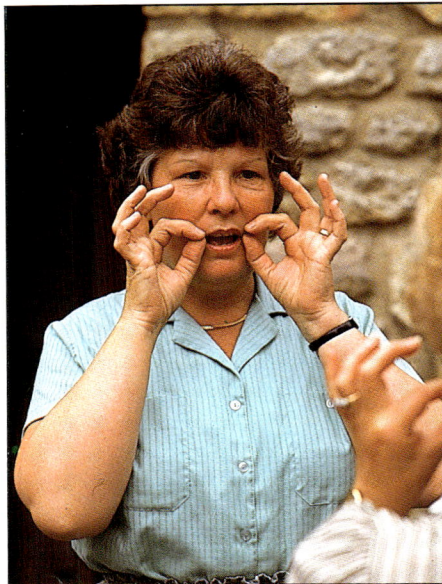

IQ tests

Intelligence is sometimes assessed by using an "IQ" or intelligence quotient test. The test shows how good a person is at using words. It may test their number skills and will certainly test their ability to reason. It will also test their ability to recognize patterns. The average IQ score is 100 with most people scoring between 85 and 115. Only 1 per cent of the population scores over 150. IQ tests are used for both adults and children but children's tests are adjusted to take their ages into account.

Sex and reproduction

- *The uterus or womb is about the size and shape of a pear.*

- *The epididymus is more than 6 m long.*

- *A baby girl is born with more than 40,000 immature eggs in her ovaries.*

- *The tendency to have twins is an inherited characteristic. This means it runs in families.*

- *A baby is usually born 38 weeks after conception.*

- *A human sperm is about 0.05 mm long; an ovum is about 0.1-0.2 mm in diameter.*

Every human being begins life as just one cell. This cell is formed when a sperm from the father joins with an egg from the mother. Protected inside the mother's body, the new cell grows and divides until eventually it has developed into a fully-formed baby. After nine months the baby is ready to be born and begin its own separate life in the world outside.

The child will resemble both its parents, for each one passes on some of their characteristics to the child. These characteristics are transferred to the child in genes which form part of the sperm and egg.

The combination of each child's genes is unique and, with the exception of identical twins, no two people on Earth are exactly alike.

► Only a few days old, a baby comes home for the first time. She will probably grow up to look much like her parents, because she shares their genes. These will determine, for example, the colour of her eyes, her hair and her skin.

The sex organs

Female

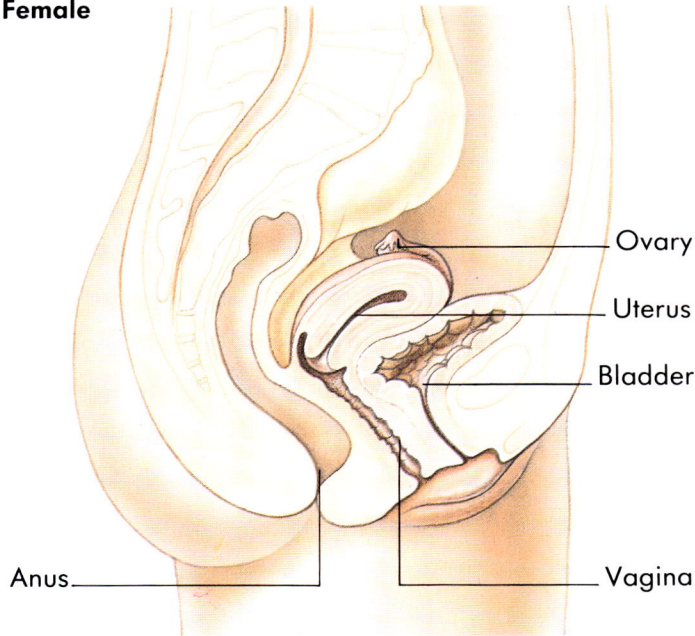

- Ovary
- Uterus
- Bladder
- Anus
- Vagina

Male

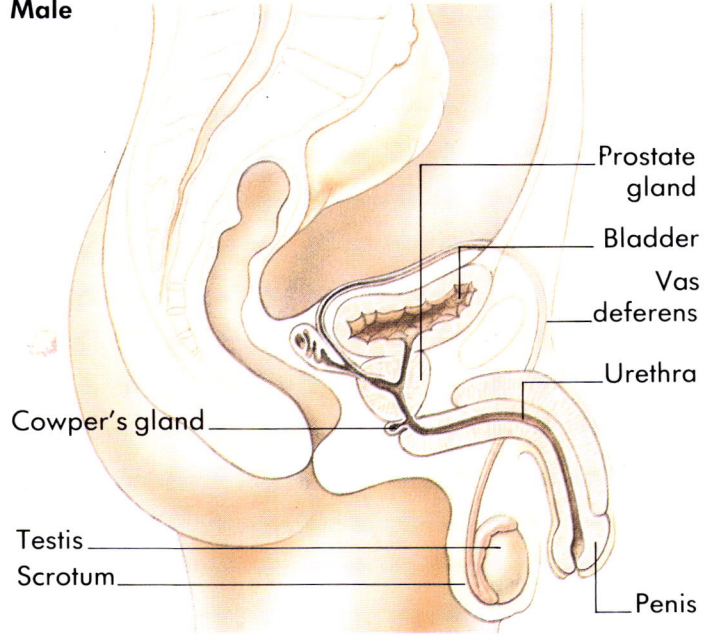

- Prostate gland
- Bladder
- Vas deferens
- Urethra
- Cowper's gland
- Testis
- Scrotum
- Penis

▲ The ovaries are situated inside the pelvis. The ova they produce move into the oviduct and pass down to the uterus. The uterus is hollow with strong muscular walls and a rich supply of blood vessels. The vagina leads from the uterus to the outside.

▲ Sperm are produced in the testes which are held just outside the body in the scrotum. Sperm pass up the vas deferens and along the urethra to leave the body through the penis. The prostate and Cowper's gland produce seminal fluid.

Sperm are made in a man's testes. Every day a man will produce three hundred million sperm cells. The sperm mature in the epididymus and pass into the vas deferens where they are mixed with fluids from nearby glands. Together the sperm and fluids are known as semen. An egg, or ovum, is released from a woman's ovaries approximately once each month in a process called ovulation. The ovum travels down the oviduct, a narrow tube, towards the uterus.

During sexual intercourse, the man's penis becomes firm and fits into the woman's vagina. Here, about 4 ml of semen, containing around 300 million sperm, is released. The sperm swim into the uterus and up into the oviducts. If a sperm should meet an ovum here, the two may fuse to form a new single cell. This process is called fertilization.

▶ During sexual intercourse sperm travel out of the penis in semen and are deposited just below the uterus in the woman's body. The sperm must then travel a further 10 cm or so to the oviduct, where there may be an ovum.

Sexual intercourse

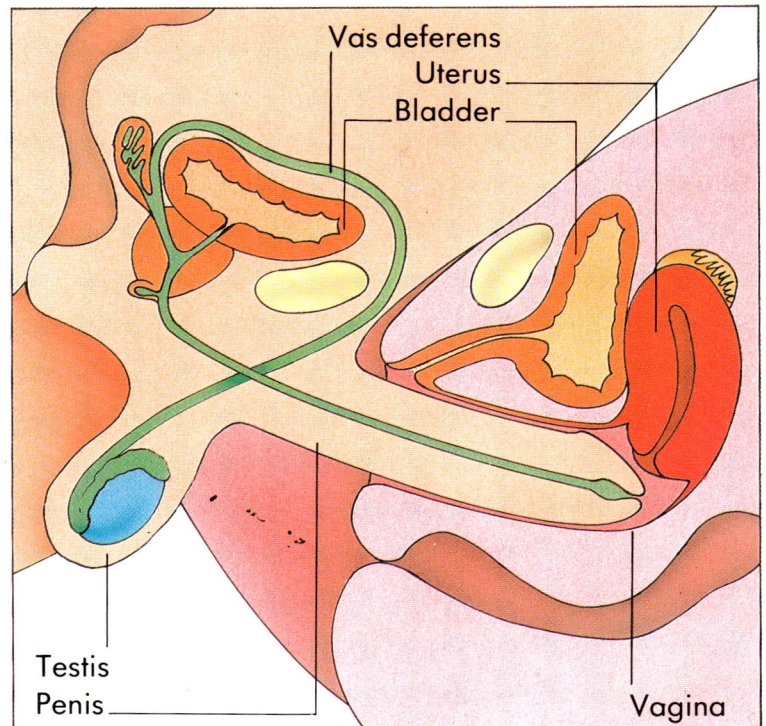

- Vas deferens
- Uterus
- Bladder
- Testis
- Penis
- Vagina

Sex cells and fertilization

Semen released during sexual intercourse contains millions of sperm, most of which die on the journey through the woman's body. A few hundred sperm may reach the ovum, but only one will be able to penetrate its outer membrane. At this moment the ovum becomes fertilized and the two cells fuse into one.

Sperm are the smallest cells in the body. Each one is tadpole-shaped with a small head and a long thrashing tail. Ova are much larger. Both sperm and ovum contain genetic material called chromosomes, which carry information determining the characteristics each parent passes to the child.

Chromosomes contain a chemical called deoxyribonucleic acid, or DNA for short. Every cell in the body, except sperm and ova, have a set of 46 chromosomes arranged in 23 pairs. However, sperm and ova have only 23 chromosomes each, one of each of the pairs. When the sperm fertilizes the ovum their chromosomes pair up to form a complete set of 46.

Each member of the chromosome pair looks the same as its partner, except for the 23rd pair which are different sizes. Because of their appearance they are called the x- and y-chromosomes and it is these which determine whether a person is male or female.

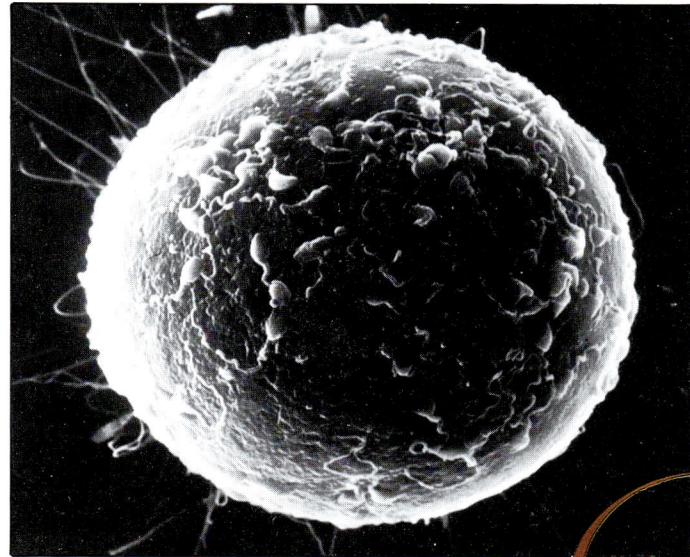

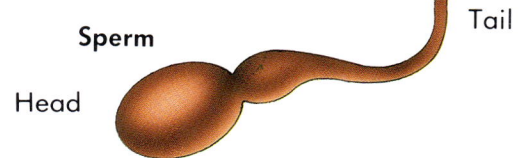

Sperm

Tail

Head

▲ An ovum, surrounded by sperm. An ovum is the largest cell in the body, between 0.1 and 0.2 mm in diameter. Each sperm is 0.05 mm long and consists of a head, which contains its chromosomes, and a tail. Only one sperm will penetrate the outer membrane and enter the ovum, leaving its tail behind.

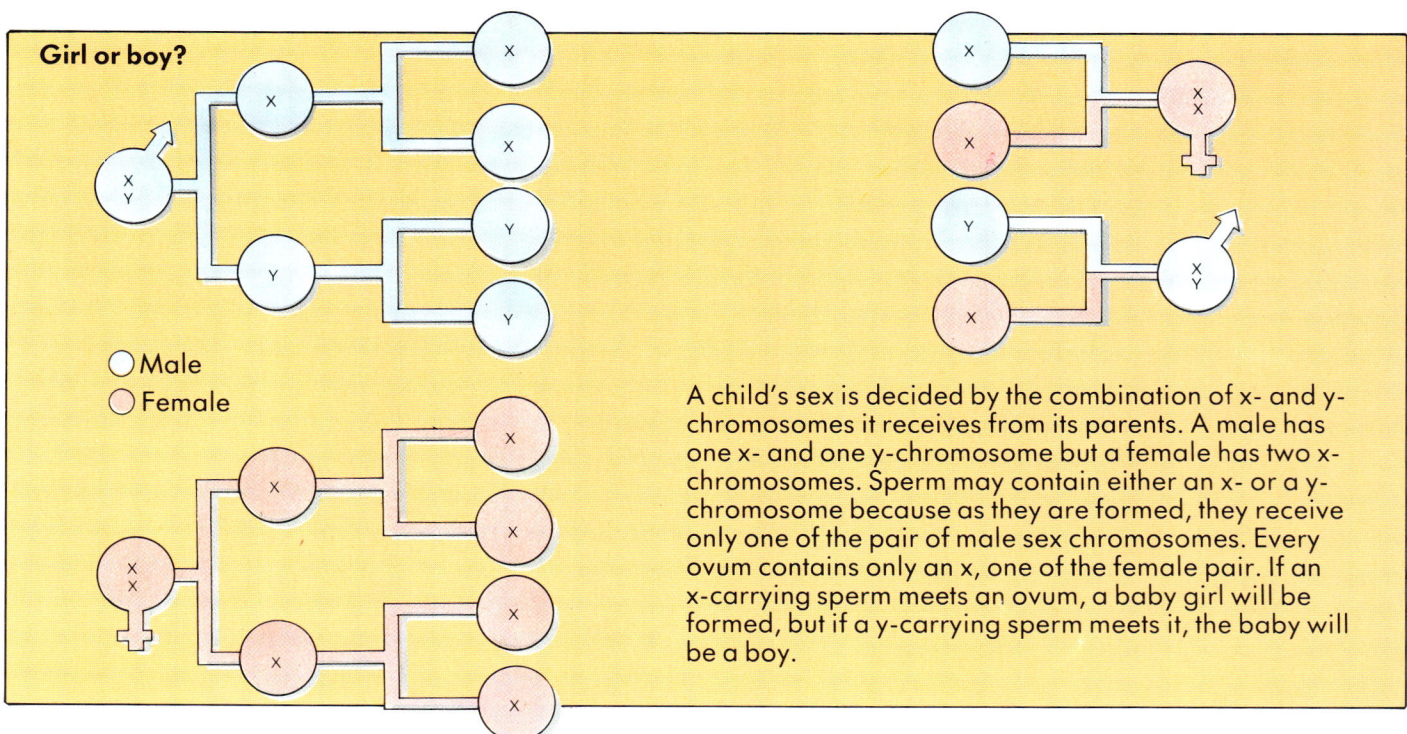

Girl or boy?

○ Male
○ Female

A child's sex is decided by the combination of x- and y-chromosomes it receives from its parents. A male has one x- and one y-chromosome but a female has two x-chromosomes. Sperm may contain either an x- or a y-chromosome because as they are formed, they receive only one of the pair of male sex chromosomes. Every ovum contains only an x, one of the female pair. If an x-carrying sperm meets an ovum, a baby girl will be formed, but if a y-carrying sperm meets it, the baby will be a boy.

Every chromosome strand is made up of thousands of units of DNA arranged in millions of different combinations. The combinations form coded instructions which are called genes.

Every cell in a person's body contains an identical set of genes. These contain all the information the cell needs to keep it going and they determine all the person's characteristics. These range from the colour of their hair, eyes and skin, to their height and ability to resist diseases.

There are millions of genes and an even greater number of possible combinations of them. So, with the exception of identical twins, no two people have exactly the same genes. This means that no two people in the world are exactly the same. Every one of us has inherited our own unique combination from our parents.

Although many of our features are inherited, not everything about us is determined by our genes. Where and how we live, our diet, and many other factors also play a part. All these things can influence a person's personality and even their physical features. For example, height and weight are partly decided by the size of a person's parents, but a particular diet and exercise programme could increase a person's size considerably.

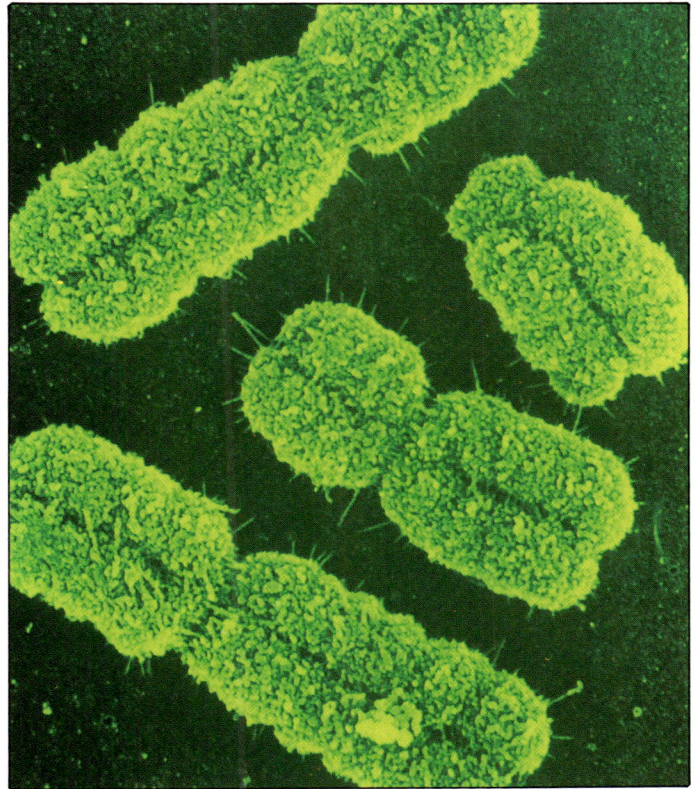

▲ This is a group of human chromosomes. The thread-like structures in the cell nucleus carry genetic information in the form of genes. Each chromosome is made up of two linked strands.

Inheriting eye colour

Eye colour is determined by a gene that comes in two different versions, "brown eye" genes and "blue eye" genes. The genes which produce brown eyes are said to be dominant over "blue eye" genes because a person who has one copy of each gene will have brown eyes. To have blue eyes a person must inherit two "blue eye" genes, one from each of their parents. Brown-eyed people, on the other hand, may either have two "brown eye" genes or one "brown eye" and one "blue eye" gene. For this reason it is possible for two brown-eyed parents, who both have one of each gene, to have children with blue eyes. Other characteristics linked to dominant genes are inherited in the same way.

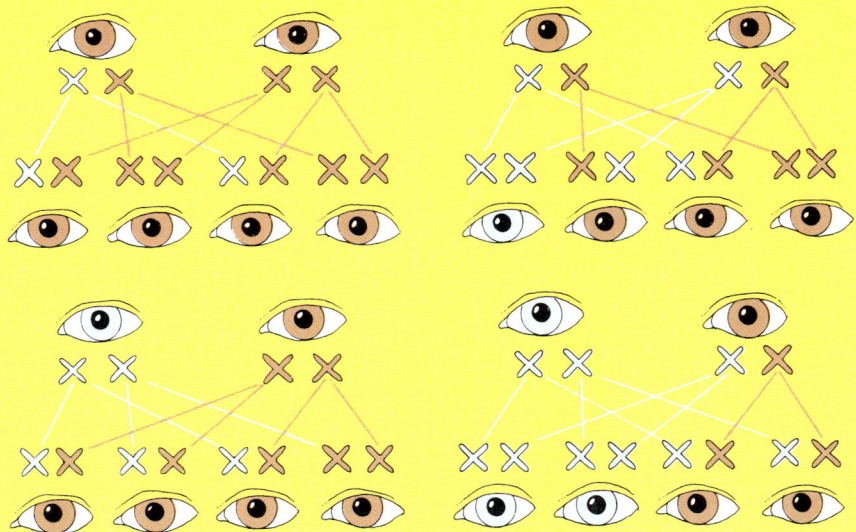

Pregnancy and birth

Pregnancy

Once an ovum has been fertilized it floats down the oviduct to settle in the uterus. It begins to grow and develop and by the time seven or eight days have passed a ball of more than 100 cells has formed. At first the cells are all alike, but gradually they change and begin to form the baby's muscles, bones, blood and heart. Two months after fertilization, all the major organs are in place, even though the baby is still only 25 mm long. For the next seven months, the baby continues to grow. It receives nourishment from its mother through the umbilical cord and it floats in a protective bag of fluid. Nine months after the ovum was fertilized, a fully-formed baby, about 500 mm long and weighing around 3.5 kg is ready to be born.

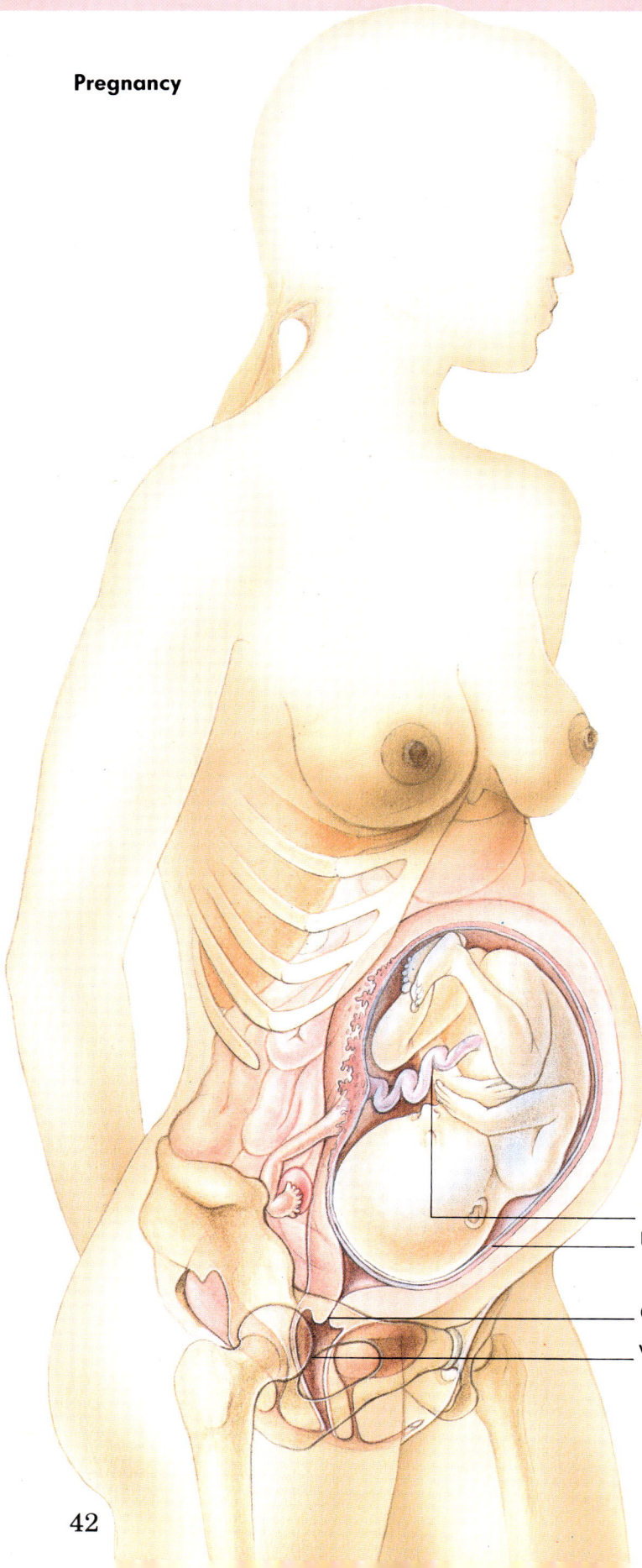

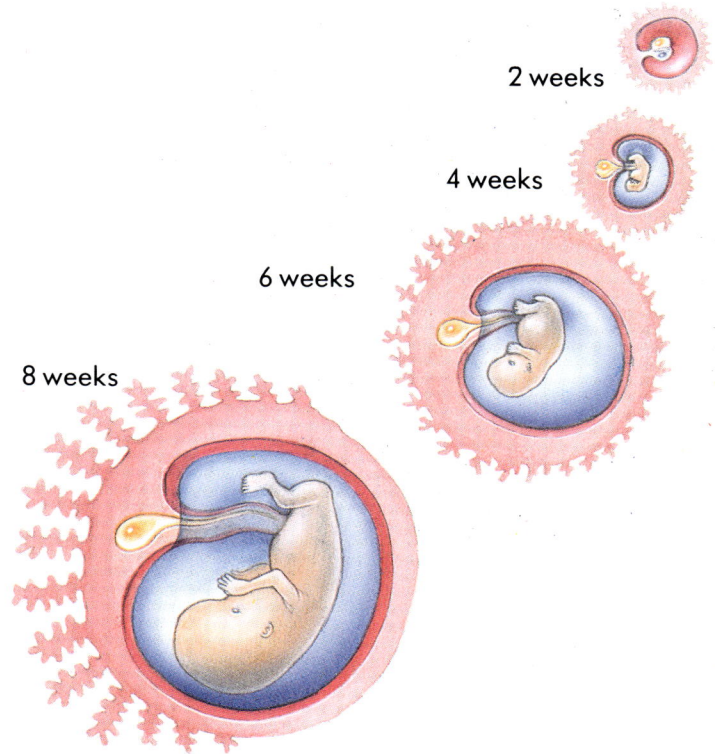

2 weeks

4 weeks

6 weeks

8 weeks

Umbilical cord
Uterus

Cervix

Vagina

◄▲ At two weeks, the developing baby is simply a flat disc of cells, but by 4 weeks the buds of tiny limbs have formed. At 6 weeks most of the baby's internal organs are in place and by 8 weeks the baby has fingers and toes. By the time nine months have passed, the baby is very cramped inside its mother's body. Most babies settle in a head down position ready to be born.

The stages of childbirth

1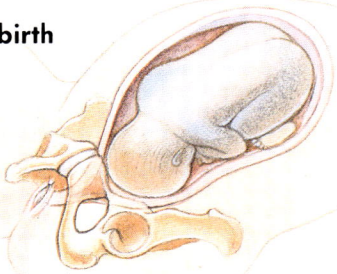

2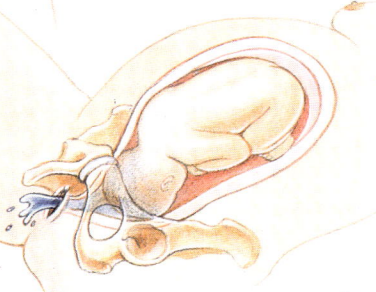

3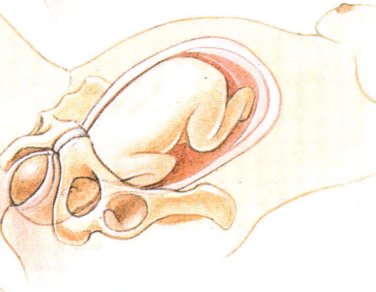

4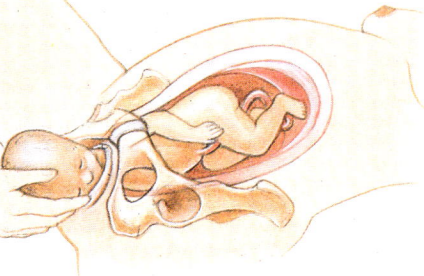

5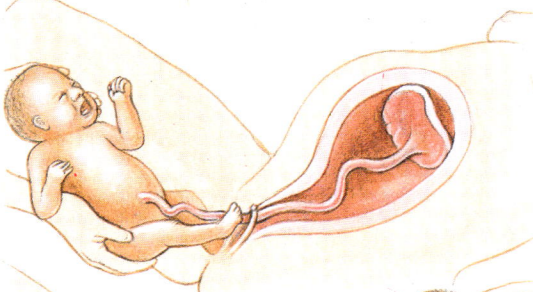

6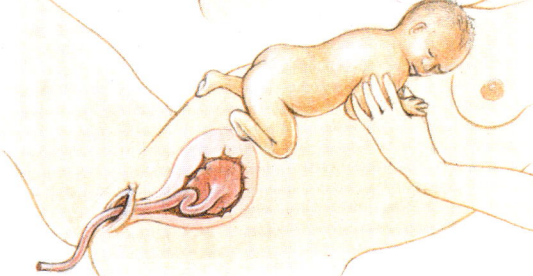

When the baby's development is complete, the mother's glands release hormones that control its birth. Birth is a very tiring event for both mother and baby and takes about 12 hours on average. Labour is the longest stage of the birth process. It begins when the mother's hormones stimulate the muscles of the uterus to contract. Gradually the neck of the uterus widens so that the baby's head can pass through. Powerful contractions continue and push the baby out of the uterus until, finally, the baby's head emerges into the outside world. After a few more contractions the baby is born and begins life on its own. However, a newborn baby is completely helpless and relies on its mother for food and warmth.

◀ (1) The neck of the uterus widens to about 10 cm.
(2) At some stage, the bag of protective fluid bursts.
(3) and (4) The baby's head is pushed down the vagina.
(5) and (6) The baby is born and the umbilical cord that joined the baby to its mother is cut.

▼ Breast milk is a perfect baby food. It contains all the nourishment a new baby needs and it is available at the correct temperature whenever the baby sucks. The milk also helps to protect the baby from colds and other illnesses. Some babies are bottle-fed on artificial milks which are imitations of human milk.

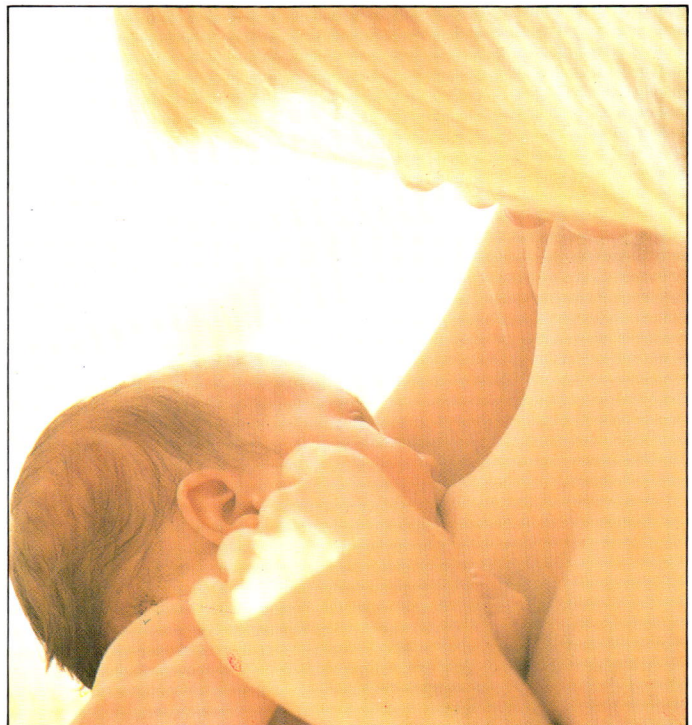

Glossary

Adam's apple The name given to the piece of cartilage that sticks out in front of the larynx. A man's Adam's apple is larger than a woman's because his vocal cords and larynx are larger.

alveoli The tiny air sacs in the lungs where oxygen is collected by the blood.

aorta The main artery which leaves the left ventricle of the heart.

artery Any blood vessel that carries blood away from the heart. The largest artery is the aorta which is 2.5 cm across.

atrium One of the two upper chambers of the heart.

axon The long fibre of a nerve cell (neurone) which carries messages to and from the cell.

bacteria Microscopic, one-celled organisms. Most bacteria are harmless but a few can cause diseases such as tetanus, pneumonia and tuberculosis.

biceps The muscle in the upper arm which contracts to bend the arm upwards.

bile A green liquid produced by the liver which helps to digest fat in the small intestine.

bladder A muscular bag which collects urine from the kidneys.

blood pressure Blood presssure depends on how strongly the heart pumps and how much the blood vessels resist the blood flowing in them.

bronchus One of the two branches of the windpipe, or trachea, which lead into the lungs. The left bronchus is about 2.5 cm long but the right bronchus is about twice this length.

canines Pointed side teeth on each side of the incisors. They are also called eye teeth.

capillary A tiny blood vessel which connects the small branches of arteries to small branches of veins.

cardiac Of the heart. For example, cardiac muscle is the muscle of the heart.

cartilage Soft smooth white tissue which covers the ends of bones at the joints. It reduces friction between the two bones which form the joint.

cerebellum The area of the brain which coordinates and controls movement.

chromosome One of the 46 bodies containing DNA that are found in the nucleus of every cell in the body. Chromosomes carry genes which determine all the body's inherited characteristics.

circulation A general name given to the body's transport system. It consists of arteries, veins and capillaries and the blood which flows through them.

cochlea The snail-shaped part of the inner ear which contains the receptors for hearing.

cornea The transparent front layer of the eyeball. It allows light to enter the eye and helps to focus light rays on the retina.

coronary Referring to the blood vessels which supply the heart. Coronary arteries cover the surface of the heart and provide food and oxygen for heart muscle. The word is also sometimes used to mean a heart attack.

cortex The outer layer of the brain which is sometimes called "grey matter". It is made of millions of nerve cells and is responsible for thinking.

dendrite One of the short fibres which carries messages towards a nerve cell body.

dentine The bone-like material inside a tooth. It is covered by a hard, protective layer of enamel.

dermis The lower layer of the skin which contains nerves, blood vessels and sweat glands.

diabetes A condition in which the body is unable to control the level of sugars in the blood. It is usually caused by having insufficient of the hormone insulin.

dialysis A method of purifying the blood when a patient has diseased kidneys. It involves filtering the blood though a dialysis machine.

diaphragm The flat sheet of muscle which separates the chest cavity from the abdomen. As the diaphragm flattens, air is drawn into the lungs. As it arches upwards, air is forced out.

DNA Deoxyribonucleic acid is a very complicated chemical which makes up the chromosomes. Different combinations of DNA make up genes which determine a person's characteristics.

eardrum The membrane at the end of the ear canal. It vibrates and passes on its vibrations to the inner ear where receptor cells respond and send messages to the brain.

enamel The hard protective covering over every tooth.

endocrine gland A gland which produces one or more hormones.

enzymes Chemical substances found in the body which speed up vital processes such as digestion and respiration.

epiglottis A small flap of cartilage which covers the entrance to the trachea as a person swallows and prevents food going down the "wrong way".

faeces Waste material which leaves the body after food has been digested.

femur The thigh bone, the largest

bone in the body.

fertilization The fusion of an ovum and a sperm. After the ovum has been fertilized it can begin to develop into a baby.

gall bladder A small sac under the liver where bile is stored before being released into the intestine.

haemoglobin The red substance found in red blood cells which gives blood its colour and carries oxygen from the lungs to all parts of the body.

hormones The body's chemical messengers which control many processes such as growth and the amount of sugar in the blood.

incisors Flat front teeth which are used to bite off pieces of food.

intestine The long tube in which food is digested. It begins at the stomach and ends at the anus.

iris The coloured part of the eye which surrounds the pupil.

kidney The two kidneys filter the blood and produce urine. They are found one on each side of the backbone just below the ribs.

larynx The voice box which contains the vocal cords. Air from the lungs makes the cords vibrate and muscles change the length of the cords to produce different sounds.

liver The body's largest organ. It controls the level of sugar in the blood, processes proteins and produces bile.

lymph A clear liquid containing white blood cells which flows through the lymph system. It helps fight disease.

lymphocyte A type of white blood cell which produces antibodies.

marrow The soft jelly-like substance in the centre of certain bones. It contains developing red and white blood cells as well as fat and blood vessels.

medulla The base of the brain which joins the spinal cord.

melanin The dark pigment which gives colour to skin, hair and eyes.

molar A large flat tooth at the back of the mouth used for grinding food.

myelin A fatty substance which insulates nerve fibres so that nerve impulses do not go astray.

nerves Bundles of long fibres which extend from neurones. Nerves carry electrical messages to and from the brain and spinal cord.

neurone A nerve cell.

ovaries The two female organs which produce ova.

pancreas The 15 cm long gland behind the stomach which produces the hormone insulin and pancreatic enzymes. Insulin controls the body's blood sugar level and pancreatic juice helps to digest food in the intestine.

pituitary gland The gland at the base of the brain which is often called the "master gland" because it controls the activities of many other glands.

pulse The throbbing that can be felt in the arteries as the heart contracts. The strongest pulse can be felt at the wrist and in the neck.

pupil The hole in the centre of the iris through which light can enter the eye.

red blood cells Small disc-shaped cells in blood which carry oxygen all around the body. Red blood cells contain haemoglobin which gives them their colour.

reflex action An action which cannot be controlled by thinking about it. Examples include the knee jerk reflex and the opening and closing of the pupil in bright and dim light.

retina The light-sensitive layer which lines the inside of the eyeball. It contains light-sensitive cells which respond to light by sending messages to the brain.

saliva The liquid produced by glands in the mouth. It moistens food to assist swallowing and it contains an enzyme which begins to digest the food.

stroke Damage to the brain caused by an interruption to the flow of blood. Part of the brain may die and a stroke can cause paralysis or loss of the power of speech.

sperm The male sex cells which are produced in a man's testes.

spinal cord A thick cord of nerves which begins at the base of the brain and extends to the bottom of the back. Nerves which branch from the spinal cord carry messages to all parts of the body.

testes The two male glands which produce both sperm and male hormones.

trachea The windpipe which leads from the throat to the two bronchi in the chest.

ureters The tubes which carry urine from the kidneys to the bladder. Each one is about 30 cm long but only 0.01 cm wide.

vagina The passageway from the uterus to the outside of a woman's body.

ventricle One of the two lower chambers of the heart. The right ventricle pumps blood to the lungs while the stronger, left ventricle pumps blood all round the body.

vitamins A group of substances which are needed to keep the body healthy. The body cannot make vitamins so they must be eaten in foods.

Index

learning 36-37
lens *28*
ligaments 10
liver *18*, 20, 22, *22*, 24, *24*
lumbar bones *8*
lungs 16, *16*, 17, *17*, 18, *18*
lymph 15, *15*, 23

M

medulla, of brain *30*
medulla, of kidney 25
melanin 7
memory 33, 36-37
meninges 33, *33*
meningitis 33
middle ear 28, *28*
"milk teeth" 21
mitochondria 18, *18*
molars *21*
muscles 6, 10-11, *10*, 14
myelin 27, *27*, 33

N

nephrons 25
nerve cell *27*
nerves 7, 21, 26, *27*
nervous system 27, *27*
neurones 27, 30, *33*
neuro-transmitter 27

O

oesophagus 22, *22*
olfactory nerve 30, *30*
optic nerve 28, *28*, 30, *30*
outer ear 28, *28*
ovaries 38, 39, *39*
oviduct 39, *39*, 42
ovulation 39
ovum 39, 40, 42
oxygen 12, 14, 16, 17, 19
oxy-haemoglobin 18

P

pancreas 22, *24*
pancreatic juice 23
paralysis 33
penis 39, *39*
peristalsis 22
pituitary gland *30*, 31
plasma 14, *15*
platelets *15*

potassium 9
pregnancy 42-43
pre-molars *21*
prostate gland *39*
protein 20
pulmonary artery 13, *14*
pulmonary vein *14*
pulp, of tooth *21*
pupil 28, *28*

R

reasoning 36
receptors 29
rectum 22
red blood cells 9, 12, 14, 24
reflex actions 33
renal artery 25, *25*
renal vein 25, *25*
reproduction 38-40, 42-43
respiration 16, 18
respiratory system *16*
retina 28, *28*
root, of tooth 21, *21*

S

sacral bones *8*
saliva 21
salivary glands 21, *22*
scent 29
scrotum *39*
sebaceous glands 7
semen 39, 40
senses 28-29
sensory areas *32*
semi-circular canals 28, *28*
sex 38-39
sex organs 39, *39*
sexual intercourse 39, *39*
sight 28
sign language 37
skeleton 6, 8-9, *8*
skin 6, 7
skull 8, 9, *9*, 30
small intestine 22, *22*, 24, *24*
sperm 38, 39, 40, *40*
spinal cord 27, *27*, 30, *30*, 33
spinal nerves 27, *27*
spine 8, *8*
stirrup bone 8
stomach 22, *22*, *24*
stroke 32
sugar 24
sweat gland *7*
sweating 25
synovial membrane 11, *11*

T

taste 29
    receptors *29*
taste buds 29, *29*
teeth 21, *21*
tendons 11
testes 39, *39*
thoracic bones *8*
tibia *11*
tongue *17*, *22*, 29
toothache 21
touch 29
trachea *16*, 17
triceps *10*
twins 38

U

umbilical cord 42, *42*, 43
urea 24, 25
ureter 25, *25*
urethra *39*
urine 25
uterus 38, 39, *39*, 42, *42*, 43

V

vagina 39, *39*, *42*, 43
valves 13, *13*
vas deferens 39, *39*
veins 13, *13*, *14*
ventricles, of brain *33*
ventricles, of heart 14, *14*
venules 13
viruses 14, 33
vitamins 23
vocal cords *17*

W

waste disposal 13, 20
white blood cells 12, 14
windpipe 16, *17*
wisdom teeth 21
womb *see uterus*

X

x-chromosome 40

Y

y-chromosome 40

Further Reading

The Human Body by Ruth and Bertel Bruun (Kingfisher Books, 1985)
Exploring Ourselves by Ed Catherall (Wayland, 1990)
Body Changes by Christine Green (Wayland, 1990)
Growing into Sex by Christine Green (Wayland, 1990)
How Your Body Works by Hindley & Rawson (Usborne, 1975)
Human Development series (Wayland)
The Body and How it Works by Steve Parker (Dorling Kindersley, 1987)
The Don't Spoil your Body Book by Claire Rayner (Bodley Head, 1989)
Pocket Book of the Human Body by Brenda Walpole (Kingfisher Books, 1987)
Heart and Blood by Brian Ward (Franklin Watts, 1982)
The Lungs and Breathing by Brian Ward (Franklin Watts, 1988) and others in this
   series, The Human Body.